CASE STUDIES IN
CULTURAL ANTHROPOLOGY

GENERAL EDITORS
George and Louise Spindler
STANFORD UNIVERSITY

HENDERSON, LOUISIANA

Cultural Adaptation in a Cajun Community

HENDERSON, LOUISIANA

Cultural Adaptation in a Cajun Community

By

MARJORIE R. ESMAN

Louisiana State University

HOLT, RINEHART AND WINSTON

NEW YORK   CHICAGO   SAN FRANCISCO   PHILADELPHIA
MONTREAL   TORONTO   LONDON   SYDNEY
TOKYO   MEXICO CITY   RIO DE JANEIRO   MADRID

Cover photo: *Agnes Huval, owner of Pat's Waterfront Restaurant, cooking crawfish at her restaurant.*

Library of Congress Cataloging in Publication Data

Esman, Marjorie R.
  Henderson, Louisiana: cultural adaptation
in a Cajun community.

  (Case studies in anthropology)
  Bibliography: p. 133
  Includes index.
  1. Cajuns—Louisiana—Henderson—Social
conditions.   2. Henderson (La.)—Social con-
ditions.   3. Henderson (La.)—Social life and
customs.   4. Tourist trade—Louisiana—
Henderson.   I. Title.   II. Series.
F379.H46E86   1985   305.7'41'076348   85-5510
ISBN 0-03-002848-5

Copyright © 1985 by CBS College Publishing
Address correspondence to:
383 Madison Avenue
New York, N.Y. 10017
All rights reserved
Printed in the United States of America
Published simultaneously in Canada

5 6 7 8   016   9 8 7 6 5 4 3 2 1

CBS COLLEGE PUBLISHING
Holt, Rinehart and Winston
The Dryden Press
Saunders College Publishing

*For Max
and
for Michael*

Foreword

ABOUT THE SERIES

These case studies in cultural anthropology are designed to bring to students, in beginning and intermediate courses in the social sciences, insights into the richness and complexity of human life as it is lived in different ways and in different places. They are written by men and women who have lived in the societies they write about and who are professionally trained as observers and interpreters of human behavior. The authors are also teachers, and in writing their books they have kept the students who will read them foremost in their minds. It is our belief that when an understanding of ways of life very different from one's own is gained, abstractions and generalizations about social structure, cultural values, subsistence techniques, and the other universal categories of human social behavior become meaningful.

ABOUT THE AUTHOR

Marjorie R. Esman received her Ph.D. in anthropology from Tulane University in 1981. Her areas of research interest have included ethnic assertion and nationalist movements and the interaction between symbols and politics. She has published several works in professional and popular journals about various aspects of Cajun life; and she has taught anthropology at Texas Christian University, the University of Southwestern Louisiana, and Louisiana State University. As an outgrowth of her interest in nationalist movements, she is currently studying Comparative Law at Tulane University's School of Law.

ABOUT THE BOOK

Henderson, Louisiana is one of the many places in the United States where there is a culturally distinctive local population. Henderson is a community of Cajuns (Acadians in more polite but less common terminology), one of the most distinctive and one of the oldest North American minorities. Originally forced out of French Canada by the British in 1755, the Acadians found a refuge in rural south Louisiana and have flourished there. Now mixed with other immigrants to the area, the Cajuns maintain an ethnic identity that is publicly reasserted in many ways, including a biennial Crawfish Festival at Breaux Bridge (near Henderson). But the more important reaffirmations of identity are private. They occur in everyday life within the community as people go about being Cajun in speech, mannerisms, philosophy of life, and the display of attitudes toward one another and toward outsiders.

Attitudes toward outsiders have become particularly important as the tourist trade has burgeoned. Tourists are kept in certain tracks, as tourists are everywhere. They are looking for something different, something interesting to see, a feeling of having had at least a small adventure. The Cajuns of Henderson and other communities of the area see to it that tourists have something different to experience. This sometimes requires a manipulation of local culture, because Cajuns are adopting many attributes of the outside, superordinate society. Cajuns in Henderson have developed complex ways of dealing with their own changing lives and the expectations of their tourist visitors.

Tourism in Henderson as elsewhere has the effect of reinforcing the ethnicity that makes the touristic experience worthwhile. Cajun culture is highlighted as a touristic experience, but it persists, as well, as a genuine, culturally distinctive way of life. Tourism reminds Cajuns that their own culture is important, and it permits them to live their private lives as they choose.

Not all, or even the majority, of Cajuns in Henderson are directly involved in the tourist trade. They work in the oil industry that became big during the 1950s and in construction; they farm, and they fish, and they hunt. There is still subsistence in the earth and the swamps and waterways. Crawfishing in particular is now big business, in addition to being a source of food. Crawfish (crayfish outside) are not only caught in their natural swamp habitat, but they are now cultivated in artificial ponds where they can be harvested more easily and their growth cycles can be more readily controlled.

The people of Henderson are flexible and adaptive. Most men can do carpentry, plumbing, welding, and other construction-type chores. Women can do the whole complex range of domestic tasks and many now hold outside jobs as well. Nearly everyone knows how to farm, garden, fish, and hunt. This flexibility and wide range of subsistence skills have stood them in good stead when times are poor or the latest economic boom fizzles in the surrounding economy.

Marjorie Esman has given us a view of Henderson and its inhabitants that no tourist will ever see. She is a resident of the area, speaks the local dialect of French, and is accepted as a friendly, trustworthy person who is writing a book about Henderson and the Cajun way of life.

We are fortunate to have *Henderson, Louisiana: Cultural Adaptation in a Cajun Community* in the CSCA series. There have been 30 case studies on nonnative communities or groups in the United States published in the series. Well before studying "at home" became acceptable, even popular, for anthropologists, Holt, Rinehart and Winston began publishing ethnographies of American life. Today it is clear that studying at home is as credible as doing fieldwork abroad. Our recent review, "Anthropologists View American Culture," in the *Annual Review of Anthropology*, 1983, identified 161 articles or books on American culture written by anthropologists—and we did not even attempt to be exhaustive. The diversity within contemporary U.S. society is as great as that contained within any comparable land mass in the world. This diversity is made all the more interesting as an object of anthropological study, because somehow the parts do interact within the whole in a surprisingly effective manner. There is a dialogue about ethnicity, social class, and the mainstream and the traditional ideology of our culture that is not well understood but that seems to work, and we are all engaged in it.

The first nonnative U.S. case study in the CSCA series, Lincoln Keiser's *The Vice Lords*, appeared in 1969. It is still in print, in an expanded fieldwork edition. Applebaum, *Royal Blue* (construction workers), Williams, *On the Street Where I Lived* (a black urban neighborhood), Wong, *Chinatown* (New York City), Madsen and Guerrero, *Mexican Americans of South Texas*, Hostetler and Huntington, *The Hutterites in North America* and *Children in Amish Society*, and Daner, *Hare Krishna*, are available through Holt, Rinehart and Winston. Other studies have been reprinted by Waveland Press and Irvington Press.

GEORGE AND LOUISE SPINDLER
Series Editors
Calistoga, California

Acknowledgments

This book could not have been written without the cooperation and generous assistance of the people of the Henderson area. In order to protect their privacy, the names of most individuals and businesses have been changed. Because identities have been disguised, I cannot directly thank all those to whom I am grateful, but they know who they are and I hope they know that I appreciate their help.

George and Louise Spindler provided encouragement and many helpful comments as the work progressed and made it possible for me to complete this project in the allotted time. With characteristic good cheer, Dan Peace of Louisiana State University reproduced the photographs and Mary Lee Eggert drew the maps. Part of the research for this project was supported by a Tulane University Monroe Fellowship (1979–80).

Contents

List of Illustrations

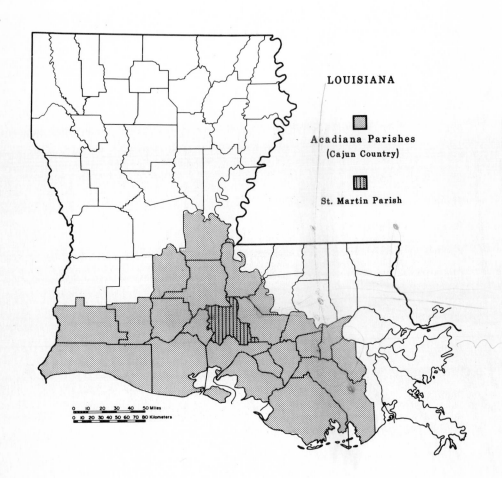

LOUISIANA

Acadiana Parishes
(Cajun Country)

St. Martin Parish

0 10 20 30 40 50 Miles

0 10 20 30 40 50 60 70 80 Kilometers

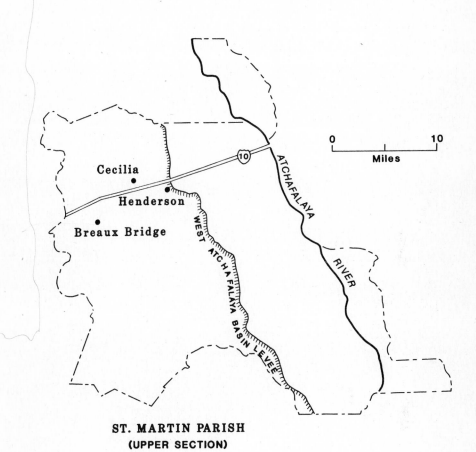

ST. MARTIN PARISH
(UPPER SECTION)

HENDERSON, LOUISIANA

1/Introduction

The Cajuns of Louisiana have long been the victims of conflicting stereotypes. On the one hand they are portrayed as virtuous, noble peasants—simple, uneducated, but goodhearted, kind, and devout. This image is heavily indebted to Henry Wadsworth Longfellow's romantic epic poem *Evangeline* (1847), which ostensibly describes the early history of these people. More recently, the early Cajuns have been described as

> simple, industrious, and kindhearted, they lived to themselves but with an open heart of justice and charity to everyone. They were a gentle race. . . . Socially they clung tenaciously to the simple manners, customs, and old French tongue of their forefathers. . . . They lived like ancient patriarchs in a state of innocence and equality (Griffin 1950:29).

On the other hand, Cajuns are often depicted as poor, ignorant swampdwellers who live in shacks, are impetuous and violent, and shun the outside world. This is the image conveyed by such movies as *The Drowning Pool* and *Southern Comfort*, by the character Rizzo in the popular television series *MASH*, and by many other portrayals in popular media and commerce.

Underlying both of these contradictory stereotypes are the common assumptions that Cajuns are isolated and backward, and that they have not changed much in over 200 years. These assumptions are not always expressed but they are usually implied. Occasionally someone does put these thoughts into words: "The exiles from Nova Scotia [Cajuns] brought to the area a philosophy and customs that have changed very little in the past couple of hundred years" (Pirtle 1977). Whether noble or savage, Cajuns are depicted as unchanged and unchanging, a U.S. reminder of an earlier and simpler era.

Like all stereotypes, these images of Cajuns contain some truth, much fiction, and are highly romanticized. Anyone looking for a paradise lost or a vestige of pioneer lawlessness will find neither among the Cajuns. Within the past two generations, Cajuns have been transformed from self-sufficient peasant farmers and fishers to a people predominantly involved in the U.S. (and international) cash economy, particularly but not exclusively the oil industry. Once largely isolated, they are now connected with the rest of the world via airports, interstate highways, and television. Where they formerly spoke French, they are now bilingual or even monolingual English speakers. The changes in the economic base and in technological opportunities have required changes in the culture;

1

while some aspects of the traditional culture persist, many have been discarded as no longer useful in the modern world.

Yet Cajuns do remain a separate and viable ethnic group with a culture and an identity of their own. Their culture has changed to conform to the requirements of the modern world, but it bears the unique stamp of the Cajun heritage. Some observers predict the demise of Cajun culture in the face of increasing modernization and urbanization (*e.g.*, Reed 1976). Yet like the people of southern Appalachia (Hicks 1976), the Cajuns of south Louisiana are adapting many of their old ways to suit the new. This study is an examination of one Cajun community and the way it has preserved its identity while making the transition from tradition to the modern world.

The fieldwork for this study was carried out over a long period of time, from 1979 until the spring of 1984. In August of 1979 I settled in a community adjacent to Henderson to conduct research for my Ph.D. dissertation. That project did not directly involve Henderson, and I did not expect to expend very much effort in the Henderson area. However, the topic of my dissertation (the Breaux Bridge Crawfish Festival) turned out to be closely linked with the economic base of Henderson (crawfish), and I ended up spending quite a bit of time with fishermen and others in the crawfish industry in Henderson. I completed my dissertation on Breaux Bridge but felt that I should eventually conduct more in-depth research in Henderson. This feeling was compounded by an awareness that Henderson is a special community with a special response to the pressures of modernization. For several years I maintained active contacts with acquaintances in the Henderson area (I remained a resident of Breaux Bridge after completing my research there), continued to collect information about the community, and waited for the opportunity to devote more time to a systematic study.

That opportunity arose in the fall of 1983, at which time I devoted myself full time to the completion of this project. I maintained my residence in Breaux Bridge and drove to Henderson almost every day (a distance of about seven miles). Because I had kept up contacts there over the years, and because I lived in the next town down the road, it was relatively easy for me to reestablish myself in full-time fieldwork. My residence outside of the community was a minor inconvenience in that I was not able to observe everything that occurred in town, but it did not deter anyone from cooperating with me—in fact, it may have been an advantage in certain contexts. For example, I was not expected to take sides in local political conflicts, which I would have had to do if I had been a town resident and therefore a voter.

Henderson is a small town (1980 population 1560) and one in which a stranger is highly conspicuous. In many cases I found that people knew about me and my activities long before I met them. On several occasions I introduced myself to people I had never met by saying I was writing a book about Henderson. I was frequently met with the response, "Oh, *you're* the one who's writing that book!" On one occasion I was chatting with a friend when a young woman approached and asked me whether I had completed my book. We had never met, but she knew who I was and what I was doing. When I visited the local volunteer fire department, a young man I had never met before described my car to me in precise detail. On another occasion I spent the morning visiting a crawfish-processing plant where a woman I knew was employed. That evening I spoke with her neighbor on the phone. The neighbor knew I had been at the plant. She also knew I had recently completed a book on the history of Henderson (a project I undertook ancillary to this one), although I had not told her that myself.

For many years Henderson was perceived by outsiders as a backward swamp town (most of its residents originally came from the nearby swamps), and Henderson residents have strong feelings about being mocked and insulted. One native in his forties insists that when he was in school the children from nearby communities, equally rural, thought of Henderson kids as "swamp trash"; to this day he is bitter about his treatment by his fellow students. Henderson is still sometimes mocked, implicitly if not explicitly, in the local media. One Henderson business owner complained that the television stations of Lafayette, the nearest city, report Henderson news only when it is bad or casts an unfavorable light on the town. He says that

> they never come here when things are going well. They don't report all the city council meetings where they do their business and go home. They never come when people hold benefits for each other or do other things to help each other out. But as soon as there's a fight, those news people are all over the place with their cameras. They just make us out to be fools.

As a result, Henderson residents are very sensitive about the way others depict their community, and they tend to be quite suspicious of outsiders who ask questions. Because they are so self-conscious about their community and its image, most of them were surprised when I said I was writing a book about Henderson. Even lifelong residents asked me what there was to write about. "How can you find enough for a whole book in Henderson?" was a common reaction. A few even tried to discourage me, saying nobody would be interested anyway. But as I persevered, people began to take an interest in my project. Indeed, many Henderson residents were flattered that I would take the trouble to listen to what they had to say and write a book about them. (In fact, I wrote two books: this one and the local history.)

Yet even those residents most interested in my project sometimes had difficulty understanding that I was interested in contemporary life. This was especially true when I was working on the local history. Henderson has been in existence for 50 years, but people kept recounting the story of how it had been founded and how the residents had come from the nearby swamps. Getting information on the years in between the founding of the community and the present was difficult. Henderson residents perceive the swamp and the original founding of their community as the most important aspects of their history; they view the rest as relatively unimportant and therefore do not understand why someone else would care about it. Eventually I convinced them that I was interested not just in the past but also in the present, and that my aim was not to mock, insult, or scorn their community. I think I was successful in gaining the trust of most of the people I worked with.

Henderson residents are suspicious of outsiders not only because they are afraid of being mocked, but also because they are afraid of being exploited or cheated. Many of the older residents are illiterate because schools were scarce, distant, and inaccessible when they were children. As a result, over the years many have indeed been exploited and cheated by unscrupulous outsiders. Everyone in town knows stories of people who signed unfavorable contracts with oil companies looking to lease mineral rights or who have otherwise made unfortunate business deals they did not fully understand. This has left many Henderson residents, especially the older ones, reluctant to deal with strangers, especially strangers who ask questions.

Because of the residents' wariness of inquisitive outsiders, my four years of familiarity with the area proved to be an asset to the research. On several occasions I was called upon to provide evidence of my good intentions. These tests came in several forms, including speaking to me in the local dialect of French to see if I could understand it (I usually did) and asking me for the names of other people in town who could vouch for me. Only two people absolutely refused to talk with me, both of them elderly people living alone. (In both cases, I made my initial contact by phone. I quickly learned not to do this. Because of their concerns, many older Henderson residents prefer not to talk with strangers over the phone.)

My lengthy acquaintance with the town proved an advantage in another respect, as well. I was able to witness changes in the community that could not have been apparent to an investigator residing for the anthropologist's customary 12 months. I observed two mayoral elections and saw shifts of political factions and of the style of politics. I saw the opening and closing of several restaurants. I saw a change in the regional economy alter subsistence patterns and other aspects of life. Some of these changes took several years to unfold, and their consequences could not have been observed in a single year.

The residents of Henderson manage their identities as Cajuns and their adoption of modern conveniences with an ease that might surprise some students of culture change and contact. It will become clear that the people of Henderson are neither "typical" U.S. citizens (whatever that means) nor are they wholly exotic. They have their own adaptations and traditions, some of which are those of their U.S. mainstream neighbors and many of which are not. Henderson is a community that has been remarkably successful in retaining its identity and in incorporating innovations into its traditional culture. There are some strains, of course, but in general these developments have caused few problems. In Henderson, neither Cajun culture nor Cajun identity is likely to disappear. Other communities around the world in similar circumstances might learn from Henderson's experiences.

2 / History and background

HISTORY OF THE CAJUNS

The Cajun homeland is the lower third of the state of Louisiana, a roughly triangular territory with its apex at the center of the state and its base following the Gulf Coast. Cajun culture emerged in Louisiana and owes much of its character to local environmental and social conditions. The state of Louisiana is culturally and ethnically complex, and to say that the Cajuns live in the southern part of the state glosses over many important ethnic distinctions in both south and north. However, because this is a study of Cajuns and not of Louisiana in general, that brief description will suffice.

Cajuns are the descendants of French peasants who were exiled from Nova Scotia (then known as Acadia and now a province of Canada) in 1755. Their ancestors had migrated from northern France to the newly acquired Canadian territories in the seventeenth century, and they had lived for a century as farmers and fishers in their new land. When Britain won control over the French Canadian provinces in 1703, the French residents were perceived as enemies of the British crown and as threats to British control. Because of this, in 1755 the Acadians, as these French peasants had become known, were forcibly deported. The story of this deportation is recounted, in highly romanticized form, in Henry Wadsworth Longfellow's poem *Evangeline*, published in 1847.

Because the British had confiscated most of their possessions, the Acadians had no money or resources with which to establish themselves in a new home. After nearly a decade of wandering—during which time many went to the French Caribbean, some to France, and a few returned to Canada—a large number of Acadians made their way to Louisiana. The first sizable group came to Louisiana in 1765, though a few individuals had arrived several years earlier. They were welcomed by the resident French and later Spanish governments in New Orleans as potential developers of an otherwise undeveloped colony. The French had founded New Orleans in 1718 and had restricted their settlement largely to that city, so they were glad to have new arrivals to settle the uncolonized interior. When the Spanish took over Louisiana in 1766, they continued the French settlement patterns and the allocation of lands to the Acadians. As a result, the Acadians were settled in the rural hinterlands, where they resumed the life of farmers.

The early Acadian settlers were given tracts of land to farm and livestock and seed to begin their work. Most were settled along the banks of the Mississippi River and along the bayous (distributaries) of that river. Within a short time many had become prosperous farmers. Like other small farmers in the area, many owned small numbers of slaves to help with the farm and domestic chores. In many respects, then, the early years of Acadian habitation in Louisiana were marked by self-sufficiency and a continuation of patterns established in Canada and by other farmers in the general area.

During the American Revolution, many Acadian men fought on the side of the rebels against their old enemies, the British. Louisiana was still Spanish territory at that time, but the Acadians were glad to drive the British away and were early friends of the new U.S. government. Today many Cajuns are proud members of the Daughters or Sons of the American Revolution, despite the fact that Louisiana was not part of the United States at that time.

Although the Acadians thrived in Louisiana, they were not able to continue their lives unchanged. Cultural patterns derived from the Acadians' devout Catholicism and a general rural peasant background persisted in Louisiana, but other aspects altered considerably. In Nova Scotia the Acadians had been farmers, fishing and raising cattle to supplement their farm diets. But northern crops do not thrive in Louisiana's subtropical climate, and so adjustments had to be made in diet and in subsistence practices. Rice, cotton, and sugar cane replaced the wheat, oats, and barley grown in Nova Scotia. Because Louisiana abounds in fish and other wildlife, the Acadians soon exploited these resources as well. Fishing and trapping became full-time occupations, and in some areas Acadians took up cattle ranching. The changes in subsistence patterns triggered permanent changes in the Acadian culture.

Changes in culture were also induced by the Acadians' relative isolation. Some of these emerging culture patterns were reinforced by the subtropical climate, which itself required new adaptations. For example, kin-based *boucheries*, or communal butcherings, were necessary in order to maximize the efficiency of meat distribution. Groups of relatives would slaughter a hog donated by one family and share equally in the meat. Each week a different family contributed an animal, ensuring fresh meat for all and reducing the danger of spoilage in Louisiana's hot climate. Kin-based cooperation was also manifest in the frequent *coups de main*, or work parties, at which family members and friends cooperated in major tasks of various sorts. Most day-to-day interactions were with kin because local communities were small. Regular Saturday night dances provided a form of entertainment and a way to keep in touch with members of other communities.

After the Louisiana Purchase in 1803, Louisiana became part of an expanding Western frontier. The U.S. government opened up previously vacant lands to residents of the 13 original states, and a diverse population came to claim land and to settle in Louisiana. After Louisiana became a state in 1812, new settlement was increased as the state government sold some of its surplus unclaimed land to increase the state coffers. Many immigrants settled in Louisiana because of the availability of land and because the state government had a policy that encouraged such immigration. Most of the new settlers in Louisiana were not of French extraction, and their presence provided a new heterogeneity to the white population of the state.

For a variety of reasons, during the 1840s many Acadian farmers began to sell their fertile waterfront lands to the new settlers. Some did this because Anglo planters were willing to pay premium prices for land that could be converted to sugar plantations; others because they were unable to keep up with tax assessments and other expenses required by the government. In any event, by the middle of the nineteenth century many Acadians had left their waterfront farmlands in favor of less desirable swamp and prairie lands that were previously unclaimed. The early part of the nineteenth century, then, brought a new crop of settlers to the area, rendered the Acadians only one of a number of European-derived groups in their territory, and saw a restructuring of settlement patterns.

Settlement of the swamps required new ways of making a living and new attitudes toward nature. The swamps abound in fish and the Acadians quickly learned that fishing was the most effective way to utilize their new environment. Improved methods of shipping fish made full-time fishing profitable toward the end of the nineteenth century and led to the development of permanent fishing villages in the swamps. Other seasonal occupations included the gathering of Spanish moss (*Dendropogon usneodies*), a wild-growing plant related to the pineapple that hangs from trees, electric poles, and anything else it can cling to. Spanish moss was shipped to New Orleans where it was used for furniture stuffing. After the Civil War, lumbering became a secondary source of income for many swamp dwellers, as old plantations were converted to timberland. The fishing and lumber industries altered the nature of swamp life for most of its occupants, and within a short time a separate swamp culture had developed, based on the traditional Acadian model but adapted to swamp conditions (Comeaux 1972).

Not all Acadians moved into the swamps. Many continued their lives as farmers near the rivers and bayous on which they had originally settled, and others moved west to the prairies where they set up farms or cattle ranches. Because the most fertile land was bought by wealthy planters toward the beginning of the nineteenth century, many Acadians became sharecroppers. In general, the nineteenth century saw many Acadians reduced from relatively prosperous, self-sufficient landowning farmers to poorer laborers working for others or having to sell their products for cash in order to live.

By the middle of the nineteenth century, the Acadians had gradually been transformed into Cajuns. This occurred by virtue of cultural adaptations and the influx of new immigrants, most of whom were quickly assimilated by the older Acadian residents. (This includes many blacks. The consensus today is that local blacks are not considered Cajuns, nor do most think of themselves as Cajuns. Nonetheless, blacks and whites share virtually identical cultures, and the distinction between white Cajuns and black Cajuns is recent and in many ways artificial.) Today probably fewer than 5 percent of the Cajun population is of pure Acadian ancestry, and many who swear that they are "pure Cajun" have non-Acadian surnames. English names like Hayes, Stelly, and McGee, and German names like

Schexnayder and Wiltz, are considered just as Cajun as the original Acadian French names such as LeBlanc, Broussard, Guidry, and Theriot.

The rapid and successful assimilation of the many non-Acadian immigrants rendered the term "Acadian" technically incorrect. A new term, "Cajun," had been introduced into the area by English speakers who glossed over the word "Acadian"; the word "Cajun" is a result of the same linguistic process that produced "Injun" from "Indian." The word "Cajun" is more inclusive than "Acadian," referring not just to the original Acadian settlers and their descendants, but also to the many others who adopted the culture patterns of the Acadians in Louisiana and who merged with the Acadian population. It is therefore more appropriate to the changed Louisiana context, and its use caught on quickly. This is not to suggest that the word "Cajun" was adopted deliberately in response to changes in ethnic composition, but rather that a term already in use was legitimized and perpetuated out of a need to label a new social category.

Cajun culture as it emerged during the latter part of the nineteenth century was typical of many rural peasant populations worldwide. Cajuns were largely illiterate and lived in the self-contained, kin-based communities characteristic of peasants. Most Cajun communities were largely egalitarian, comprising an ignored underclass in the overall Louisiana and U.S. social hierarchies. They spoke a language different from that of the U.S. majority, a dialect of French that varied slightly from one community to another but that had generally evolved from the French the Acadians had spoken in Nova Scotia. Cajun French became the *lingua franca* of the area, adopted by most of the non-French immigrants, and the use of French has long been a reasonably reliable indicator of Cajun heritage. Like other peasants, rural Cajuns were generally inward-directed, politically apathetic, and conservative. Remnants of these attitudes persist today in small towns. I am acquainted with several Cajuns who keep their money at home because they do not trust bank officials. In many small communities there is more than slight mistrust of locals who have become wealthy (Gold 1978). These attitudes may have been fostered by the dominant society that ignored the Cajuns. Lacking adequate educational facilities, Cajuns were not in a position to take part in political decisions, many of which they could not understand anyway because of their separate language. Ignored by the dominant society, Cajuns were forced to rely on themselves.

This does not mean that all Cajuns were poor, isolated, and ignorant. A small indigenous elite developed in some of the towns along the bayous. Roads were poor throughout the state, and the Mississippi River and the bayous were used as major transportation routes. A few enterprising Cajuns were able to exploit the traffic for retail purposes. Many of these merchants became prosperous, educated their children (in French) at Catholic schools, became sufficiently bilingual to handle commerce with the outside, and adopted the airs and tastes of the upper middle class in New Orleans and other cities. These people became the political and social leaders of the Cajuns and served as mediators between the rural Cajun majority and the outside world.

The changes produced by the twentieth century were far more drastic than any that had occurred previously. The progressive mechanization of agriculture reduced the need for field hands and sharecroppers, and as population increased many family farms were subdivided beyond utility. Louisiana property laws require that all heirs inherit equal shares of the parental estate, so the subdivision of family property results in increasingly smaller shares being passed down. During the 1930s, as these changes were beginning to take effect, many Cajuns left their homes to work in the newly developing oil fields of Texas. Coincident with this were the reforms of Governor Huey Long, in which roads were built, schools improved, and a new awareness of the rights of the rural poor asserted. Cars, radios, electricity, movies, and later television invaded south Louisiana as elsewhere, bringing in new ideas and information previously unavailable to a rural and isolated people. In addition, Louisiana developed its own oil industry after the 1930s, making it possible for previously self-sufficient farmers and fishers to work for cash and to earn relatively high wages. By the middle of the twentieth century, then, the isolated Cajun had been led into the U.S. mainstream and had largely abandoned the self-sufficient modes of production and ways of life.

CONTEMPORARY CAJUN IDENTITY

Cajun culture had evolved during the nineteenth century as a function of a specific set of environmental, social, and political circumstances. As these conditions changed, the culture was no longer fully adapted to the prevailing circumstances. By the middle of the twentieth century, Cajuns had become aware of the benefits of education and full participation in the outside cash economy, as well as of the use of the English language. Because prestige accrued to those who were most acculturated to the U.S. mainstream, most Cajuns followed that route. In the years since World War II, there has been a sharp reduction in the number of south Louisianians who speak only French, who work on family farms or who fish for a living, and who adhere to many of the old culture patterns.

Not all former culture patterns have disappeared, however great the changes have been. Today there is a mixture of old and new, combinations of traits preserved and those recently adopted. The blend of traits varies from place to place and context to context. Though employment in oil and other industrial fields is common today, farms and fisheries remain significant contributors to local economies. Many of these operations, particularly the farms, have been transformed from small family concerns to big business. Of the few independent fishers who remain, many hold other jobs as well. Self-sufficiency has been all but abandoned. French is still spoken by most of the older people and by many of the adults over age 35, and occasionally a child enters school with only minimum competence in English, though this is becoming increasingly rare. Catholicism and family ties remain strong, as does the popularity of traditional foods. What has happened is that aspects of Cajun culture have survived in an updated form: rejected if useless, changed if necessary, and preserved where appropriate.

As a result of these changes, Cajun identity is being redefined on many levels. While the social and environmental conditions that created the group have changed, the group maintains a strong sense of its identity. A recent study revealed that Cajuns no longer consider French language or Acadian ancestry to be particularly significant to modern Cajun identity (Chafetz, Esman, and Manuel 1982). A Cajun can live in the city, work in an office, and speak only English. There are Baptist Cajuns and Cajuns who live in other states. Today the most important diagnostic of Cajun identity is represented by the contrast between Cajuns and "Americans" or non-Cajuns. The awareness that Cajuns are different from other Americans and that Cajuns live in south Louisiana has produced a strong sense of place and a deep emotional tie to their land and region.

In fact, there is currently a renewed sense of pride in Cajun identity. While at one time Cajuns were scorned as ignorant peasants, today they have acquired a certain social prestige among other Louisiana residents. Pejorative terms for Cajuns, notably the word "coonass," are now uttered with pride. (The derivation of the term "coonass" is unknown, but the word was introduced sometime after World War II as an ethnic slur.) Bumperstickers reading "You ain't done nothing till you've done it with a coonass" appear on cars throughout the region. In addition, there have been formal attempts to revive the use of French in public; these efforts have met with mixed success, especially among the most rural Cajuns, but they have helped reduce the stigma attached to the use of French. Cajun country, now known as "Acadiana," is becoming a popular tourist attraction, and Cajuns are becoming aware of the fact that they possess something that others find interesting. Cajuns have been transformed from rural peasants outside of the mainstream to full participants in U.S. life, but with a heritage and culture unique to themselves and now of interest to others.

This does not mean that Cajuns are trying to return to their former ways. They know that jobs, high incomes, and consumer goods are preferable to self-sufficiency, poverty, and deprivation, whatever the costs in cultural terms. What it means is that there is a general self-consciousness about identity (and a rapacious interest in anything written about them). Also, among a very small segment, there is a renewed interest in French education, traditional Cajun music, and other forms of expressive culture. A current movement toward bilingual education has brought French classes to many area schools. Yet few of the parents who enroll their children in these classes speak French with their children at home. French is perceived as having sentimental value but as being of little use in the modern world. Although Cajuns no longer live in the ways of their nineteenth-century ancestors, they still consider themselves to be Cajuns and feel strongly about this identity.

HENDERSON: "THE END OF THE ROAD"

The town of Henderson is located in St. Martin Parish (county), near the center of the Cajun area. It is situated at the western levee of the Atchafalaya Basin, the largest freshwater swamp in the United States and the location of the original Acadian swamp settlements. This swamp was created by the regular flooding of the Atchafalaya River, a river that drains excess waters from the Mississippi and which, someday, will capture the Mississippi. Henderson resembles what is elsewhere in Louisiana called a "line village" (Newton 1972): most of the development extends the length of the three-mile road that is the only route into and out of town. The business center and the oldest part of Henderson is located at the end of this road at the swamp levee, with the residential areas extending west of the levee along the main road. A few smaller streets have been built on both sides of the main road as population has increased, but the town is principally oriented along the one main road and clustered where the road ends.

Today Henderson is located just off a major interstate highway. It is less than 15 miles from the city of Lafayette (population roughly 90,000), the business center of the Louisiana oil industry. Baton Rouge, the state capital, is some 40 miles away, and New Orleans another 80 miles past Baton Rouge. All of these places are readily accessible by means of the new interstate highway. In addition, Henderson is just a few miles from the somewhat larger town of Breaux Bridge (population 6000), which serves as the center of commerce for a wide surrounding area. Shopping, banking, and entertainment facilities are readily available, if not in Henderson itself, then within a few miles along good roads. Although it is a small town, Henderson is by no means isolated.

This, however, was not always the case. Until the 1960s Henderson was isolated and neglected, and was in a literal sense the "end of the road." Access to the community was poor. The early residents had little money and little ability to provide themselves with many amenities. Residents in their early forties recall being teased at school because they came from such a backward place as Henderson, and remember when they had no facilities for anything at all. The heritage of isolation still affects Henderson despite the town's new accessibility and recent prosperity. Henderson therefore contains a blend of old and new and in many ways embodies most aspects of Cajun history and culture.

Most of what is now Henderson was originally swampland, uninhabited by either Indians or Europeans. The area was ignored until the middle of the nineteenth century when the Acadians left their original farmsteads and the population of Louisiana had so swelled with immigrants that previously undesirable lands were needed for settlement. As this occurred and as the fishing industry grew to permit flourishing swamp communities, the area close to what is now Henderson contained several thriving communities of swamp fishers and other swamp dwellers. None of these communities was located where Henderson is now; they were closer to the Atchafalaya River, a few miles east. Surrounding the swamp, several miles west of what is now Henderson, were successful farmsteads on dry land. What is today the community of Henderson was vacant swampland surrounded by farms until the 1930s.

In the spring of 1927, high water in the Mississippi River caused the Atchafalaya River to flood. Most of the dry land in the surrounding areas was submerged and the residents evacuated. As a result of this disaster, the U.S. Army Corps of Engineers built a new system of locks and levees designed to control the Atchafalaya River and to prevent future floods. These levees confined the swamp area to a narrower territory, causing higher water within the confines of the swamp while allowing previously flooded lands now outside the levees to drain. By creating almost permanent flood conditions between the levees, the new levees changed conditions for fish and altered the nature of the fishing industry. This, coupled with the new higher water levels within the swamp that kept the swamp villages almost permanently flooded, led to the destruction of the swamp communities. As the swampers left their ruined villages, many moved to the newly dried land adjacent to their fishing grounds. A small farming settlement near a train station at the new western levee, about a mile north of where the center of Henderson is now, attracted many of the former swampers who wanted to remain close to their original homes.

During the 1930s as the population of the small community by the train station grew, a new type of business was developed there. Within a few years of each other, two local residents established restaurant/nightclubs to serve the residents and the men who were working on the new levees. The proprietor of the older of these restaurants, a woman now in her nineties, recalls that

> we served fried fish that we bought from the fishermen, big platters for 50 cents. We also had a boarding house for the men working on the levee and we ran a small grocery store. That's all we served, just fish, but people used to come. People were poor, but they came to eat with us and at Guidry's Place [the other restaurant]. There was plenty of business for both.

These restaurants were located in an area that is now within the corporate limits of Henderson. At that time, however, Henderson as it now exists had not yet been founded. In 1934 Henry Guidry, owner of Guidry's Place restaurant and bar, needed a new location for his business because he lacked adequate garbage facilities. He moved his building to a spot on a canal (which he used as a garbage dump until his death in 1954) at the end of a dirt road leading to the new levee. The new location was somewhat less than a mile from his old one, but it was in an area that was completely uninhabited. Within a short time after he moved his restaurant there, two fish markets (one with a small grocery store attached) were built across the dirt road from Guidry's restaurant. Fisher families began to move to the new area in larger numbers as the land dried and as more services became available. By the late 1930s a small town had developed and had become known as Henderson.

Homer Melancon, owner of the first fish market and the second business to be located at Henderson, recalls that

> there was nothing here when I came, just Guidry's Place across the street there, and a couple of fishermen living nearby. I came here because there was no place else to go with my business after the fishermen moved out of Pelba [the swamp community where Melancon had lived]. I followed my fishermen to where they were living. There weren't no other businesses here besides us [the restaurant and the two fish markets] until the 1960s. We were the end of the road here.

Because Henderson was settled largely by residents of the swamp communities, the swamp continues to play an important part in the self-image of the community. The town of Atchafalaya, the largest of the old swamp communities, is especially important. The town's mayor, a leading restauranteur, currently owns two restaurants, one catering principally to tourists and one to locals.* In the

* After this book was written the mayor consolidated his two restaurants into one. In the belief that they were competing against one another, he moved the local establishment to the tourist-oriented one and opened a nightclub in place of the old local restaurant.

back courtyard of the locally oriented restaurant he has built a model of the now-defunct town of Atchafalaya. This model is not visible from the road and was not designed as a tourist attraction. It was intended to spark a nostalgic sentiment in the residents of the town, to whom Atchafalaya has a strong emotional value. The name Atchafalaya is still used by businesses in the area, and while the name may in some cases refer to the river rather than to the old community, the word "Atchafalaya" still evokes memories of the old town and stimulates local pride and sentiment. Henderson residents still identify strongly with the swamp, even after nearly 50 years of settlement on dry land.

Many of the communities in the area surrounding Henderson are little more than collections of a few houses along a road, often with a small general store serving as the focus of the settlement. Most of these are farming communities, though now they often contain people working in other occupations, as well. Henderson began as such a settlement, although one of fishers rather than farmers. The population initially was clustered adjacent to the levee at the end of the road,

A business in Henderson. The name Atchafalaya is still widely used despite the fact that the town of that name was abandoned half a century ago.

with the houses on small lots suitable for fishers with little need for land. However, over the years Henderson has incorporated some of these nearby farming communities, and today it is considerably larger than it was when it was founded. The railroad station community, where the restaurants were originally located, has long merged with the fishing settlement at the levee, and today Henderson is a town of fishers and farmers, with few local distinctions between them.

Change came slowly but definitively to the new community. The small dirt road leading to the levee was paved in 1954, making it easier to get in and out of town. During this time the economic base of the town began to change. Wage labor in nearby communities became increasingly common and Henderson residents slowly became more prosperous. The nature of the fishing industry changed dramatically during the 1960s, for reasons to be explained in Chapter 3. By 1970 Henderson was no longer strictly a poor fishing village, but it was still the end of the road.

The most dramatic changes came during the 1970s. In 1971 the small community of Henderson was incorporated into a town, with Pat Huval, the leading restaurant owner, chosen as mayor. Incorporation meant that Henderson could control its own public works, and within a short time many dirt roads were paved and new facilities constructed.

Most important, though, was the construction of a major interstate highway with an exit near Henderson. Prior to the construction of this road there was no road through the Atchafalaya swamp, and the now 40-mile trip to Baton Rouge required lengthy detours and took over two hours. Points west, although not requiring passage through the swamp, were almost equally inaccessible because Henderson residents had to take back roads to the larger city of Lafayette in order to gain access to more major highways. In 1973 the final span of the interstate was completed, with an exit near the beginning of the single Henderson main road. This new interstate exit transformed Henderson from a small town at the "end of the road" to a busy stop on a major highway.

Technically, the exit off the interstate is outside the Henderson city limits and connects to roads leading to several other communities. But the Henderson area has capitalized on the exit more than have other nearby communities. The Henderson main road extends the three-mile length between the interstate exit and the levee. The older, principal business center of Henderson is adjacent to the levee at the far end of the road, but recently a second business area has emerged at the other end near the interstate exit. The Henderson road now connects two commercial centers: the old one at the levee and the new one at the interstate. The new commercial center caters largely to intersate travellers and comprises gas and service stations, snack bars, lunch counters, fast-food establishments, and one large restaurant complex oriented toward visitors. It also contains a supermarket and other smaller shops catering to residents, but these are less numerous than the others and are not directly adjacent to the exit. This new business area is not within the corporate limits of the town of Henderson, but it is now generally considered an extension of the town by all except the older residents who remember it as a separate community.

Because of the excellent fishing and the number of professional fishers living in Henderson, fresh and inexpensive seafood has always been readily available. Cajun cooking is famous for its spicy seasonings and a wide variety of highly flavored seafood and fish dishes. Henderson has been known for its restaurants since the early days of its founding by Henry Guidry. Since the opening of the interstate the restaurant industry has grown tremendously. At this writing there are some half-dozen large restaurants, most catering primarily to tourists, and a like number of smaller, more locally oriented establishments. Restaurants now account for much of the town's employment and local revenue and the first mayor (and as of this writing the only mayor since the incorporation of the town) is a restaurant owner. Henderson has become the capital town of Cajun restaurants, famous across Louisiana and elsewhere for the abundance and the quality of its food.

The emergence of Henderson as a restaurant capital was made possible by the construction of the interstate. Once an out-of-the-way little town known for good food, Henderson is now conveniently located. People who used to make the difficult trip just to eat there can now get there more easily and those who never went because it was too inaccessible now find it a simple journey. Visitors now include families on vacation, groups or organized bus tours, and people from nearby cities who make the trip especially to eat in Henderson. As a result of the interstate, Henderson now sees thousands of outsiders a week where just a few decades ago it rarely saw anybody who didn't live there. Many of these outsiders have little impact on the town because they merely buy gas and move on, but many stay to eat and to interact with the residents. These tourists have had an important effect on the economy and on the identity and culture of the community.

Henderson has been transformed from a small settlement of poor, French-speaking fishers and farmers to a sizable community with a fairly diverse economic base. Although it remains predominantly a Cajun town, Henderson is no longer occupied exclusively by Cajuns. The interstate has made it possible for people from other areas, particularly those employed in Lafayette (a few minutes away on the new road), to settle in Henderson. In addition, the town now contains a greater ethnic diversity than it has at any other time in its history. The swampers who settled there were exclusively white, and the population of Henderson is now 88 percent white despite the fact that the surrounding farm communities have always had sizable black populations. In the mid-1970s several families of Vietnamese refugees settled in Henderson where many found employment in the growing seafood industry. Of the 12 percent nonwhite population of Henderson, half (6 percent) are black and half are Vietnamese. This has had a profound impact on the nature of the community.

Today most Henderson residents depend on commercial industries such as the seafood and restaurant industries and on the oil industry for their livings, as well as on the traditional occupations of farming and fishing. They are no longer isolated geographically or culturally from the rest of the United States. The town has become diversified, and in a literal sense it is no longer the "end of the road." Nonetheless, Henderson remains distinctively Cajun. How it has preserved its Cajun culture and identity in the face of all of these changes is the subject of the rest of this book.

3 / "The town that crawfish built"

Henderson's economy begins and ends with fish. The community was first settled by displaced swamp fishers; the first businesses there were fish restaurants and fish markets; and today the main road into town is lined with restaurants and seafood- and fish-processing plants. Henderson handles all aspects of the fish business from procurement to cuisine. In one way or another the life of Henderson revolves around the fish industry.

In the early years Henderson was a small, isolated town and even the fish industry, the main source of income for most residents, provided only a modest income. The fish most commonly caught and sold included catfish (several species), buffalofish (*Ictiobus cyprinellus*), and gaspergou (*Aplodinotus grunniens*). These fish shipped easily and had ready markets in other cities across the United States. Other varieties were used for local domestic purposes, but did not constitute part of the commercial market.

Although it might seem that fisher families would always have had enough to eat, this was not always the case. The commercial price for fish has always been low in Louisiana because of the abundant supply, and so a fisher must provide a great quantity in order to make a living. In the early years many fishers had to sell almost all of what they caught in order to make enough money to pay their bills. This was especially true during the Great Depression, when Henderson was first being established. Lionel Guidry was a fisherman when he moved his family to Henderson in the early 1930s. He eventually went to work for an oil company because he could make more money that way. He recalls that when he was fishing for a living

> lots of times we barely had enough to eat ourselves. We would sell all our fish to buy groceries. We would buy a big bag of cornmeal and eat cornbread and coush-coush [a Cajun dish made of cornmeal and milk] and beans. All that fish around us, and we couldn't eat it. You couldn't hardly make a living as a fisherman in those days.

Over the years conditions improved for fishers and their families, but the foundations of the industry remained the same until the 1960s. At that time the fish industry in Henderson and the surrounding area was dramatically transformed. Within the past two decades, Henderson's economy has come to revolve around the crawfish. This crustacean now dominates the lives of the people of the area.

17

DEVELOPMENT OF THE CRAWFISH INDUSTRY

The crawfish is a small freshwater crustacean known elsewhere in the United States as a crayfish or a mudbug. There are hundreds of species of crawfish world-wide, found on every continent except Africa. Of these hundreds of species, 29 live in Louisiana. The two species most commonly used as food in Louisiana are *Procambarus clarkii* and *Procambarus acutus acutus* (La Caze 1976:3). The craw-fish resembles a tiny lobster, normally reaching about six inches long. Crawfish live in standing water, and under wild conditions they are generally available for procurement from January until late spring (Comeaux 1972).

The edible part of the crawfish is the tail, often little more than one inch long. As with many other varieties of shellfish, crawfish must be boiled alive. The meat must be peeled from the shell after the animal has been boiled. Once the meat has been removed from the shell, it can be eaten as is or can be cooked in a wide variety of ways.

The people of south Louisiana have always been consumers of crawfish, espe-cially those who live in or near the swamps, where crawfish are plentiful. Crawfish have many advantages as a food source: they are readily available, particularly in the spring; they are easy to catch; and for a fisher they are free for the cost of a small quantity of bait. During the 1930s crawfish were so plentiful and so in-expensive that area bars served platters of boiled crawfish free with orders of beer. However, crawfish did not become important commercially for many years, and even at home they were not always the staple food that contemporary Cajuns sometimes think they were. Lionel Guidry says that even when he and his family had to struggle to find something to eat, they rarely ate crawfish:

> Those things were all over the place in those days. We had them all around the house when we lived in the swamps. But we didn't cook them all that much. I don't know why, people just didn't like them like they do now. We would eat them sometimes, but not like now. Just think, we had all that good food all around us and we didn't eat it—and if we had only known what people would pay for them now!

Nobody is entirely certain why crawfish were not as popular as a food item in the past as they are in Louisiana today. It may be because they were considered "poverty food": eaten only by people who couldn't afford to buy anything else. Indeed, individuals from more prosperous families are the ones most likely to deny having consumed crawfish prior to the 1960s; those who were less well off fre-quently acknowledge, as did Lionel Guidry, that they did eat crawfish occasionally. Also, people in other parts of the United States, including Anglo north Louisiana, generally consider crawfish unfit to eat. As a result, Cajuns who did eat crawfish were sometimes mocked by outsiders. Whatever the reason, although crawfish have always been at least a small part of the diet of the area, it was not until recently that there has been enough demand for them to constitute the basis of a commer-cial industry.

Various conditions that arose during the 1940s set the stage for the gradual emergence of a crawfish industry. The construction of the new Atchafalaya Basin levees increased flooding within the swamp while they allowed the land outside to drain. The higher water level within the swamp provided a favorable habitat for crawfish and caused a rapid increase in the crawfish supply. This made it economically feasible for crawfish to be exploited commercially, especially for restaurants that could buy large quantities. The restaurants in the new community of Henderson, located adjacent to the swamp, provided a ready market for a locally recognized and inexpensive food. In addition, during this period increasing numbers of Cajuns were moving to the cities and larger towns of the area. Many of these newly urbanized Cajuns had previously lived close to the swamps and had been occasional consumers of crawfish. Now, lacking direct access to the swamps, some were willing to buy small amounts of crawfish for the first time. For these reasons, the emergence of a crawfish industry became possible only during the 1940s.

To take advantage of the developing interest in crawfish, Ozema Allemond of Henderson began to catch crawfish and sell them live to customers from Lafayette and other surrounding places. Before long other local fishers were doing the same. By the late 1940s Homer Melancon and the other fish processor in Henderson, Shelton Peltier, had added the sale of live and boiled crawfish to their businesses. Within another few years Fernand Broussard, owner of Henderson's popular Moonlight Club, hired a few women to peel crawfish meat for him to serve in his restaurant. Shortly thereafter Melancon and Peltier both incorporated crawfish-peeling facilities into their fish-processing plants. By the mid-1950s Henderson had acquired a reputation as the center of the newly emerging and growing crawfish industry.

Broussard's club was oriented toward local residents who were already familiar with crawfish. Throughout the 1940s the market for crawfish remained largely a local one. However, in 1954 Pat Huval built a new restaurant near where Guidry's Place had been. Located adjacent to a canal with a scenic view of the swamp, Huval's restaurant began to attract not just locals but people from elsewhere. Crawfish were put on the menu at Pat's and visitors began to eat them.

Until 1960 crawfish could not be more than a seasonal item on menus or in area diets, and crawfish provided only a seasonal income for those who depended on it. The season for wild or "deepwater" crawfish is relatively short, usually limited to the spring months when the water in the Atchafalaya Basin is high due to the melting snows up north. An unusually wet spring can sometimes extend the season into late June, but it is extremely rare for crawfish season to go beyond then into midsummer. (This occurred in 1983, when crawfish were available as late as August. Many of the processors reported that they had never seen crawfish run so late in the season, and 1983 proved a record year for the industry.) In 1960 the Louisiana legislature allocated $10,000 for research into techniques of crawfish farming in order to extend the season and further develop the growing industry. The outcome of this research has greatly expanded the season for crawfish. Today cultivated crawfish can be harvested as early as October, which means that in a good year it is now possible to obtain fresh crawfish from October well into May and sometimes later (crawfish were available for almost the entire 12-month stretch from October 1982 to October 1983, with only about a six-week hiatus). Since 1960, therefore, the crawfish industry has depended heavily on cultivated crawfish. Crawfish cultivation has made it possible for crawfish processing and fishing to become full-fledged industries instead of seasonal sidelines to other fishing.

Demand for crawfish began to grow during the 1960s, due in part to the advent of cultivation and the attendant publicity. Today crawfish processors insist that they have an almost unlimited demand for their product and are constrained only by the supply, which is never adequate. Most of the crawfish is sold to restaurants and grocery stores in Louisiana, but much is shipped to other states, especially Texas, where many Cajuns now live.

Since the advent of large-scale crawfish cultivation, crawfish procurement and processing have become the principal activities of the fish industry in Henderson and throughout St. Martin Parish. Between 1963 and 1970 much of the wooded area surrounding Henderson was converted to crawfish ponds and was in active production. From 1960 to 1982 the number of crawfish-processing plants in St. Martin Parish increased from five to 26, with 14 of these located in Henderson. The state of Louisiana had 40 crawfish plants in 1982, meaning that the little town of Henderson alone had more than one-third of the state's total number of crawfish plants.

Today there are only three fish-processing plants in Henderson that deal with the traditional catfish, gaspergou, and buffalofish, and one that deals exclusively with catfish. Except for the catfish plant, the plants that handle the traditional varieties of fish also deal in crawfish and depend heavily on crawfish for several months of the year. Several of the crawfish plants now handle crabs as well, because the equipment and the techniques for processing crawfish and crabs are virtually identical, and by handling both a plant can stay in operation almost year-round. However, most of these plants view crabs as a sideline and crawfish as the mainstay of the business, though one Henderson plant handles crabs preferentially and crawfish as a sideline. The emergence of the crawfish industry has transformed Henderson from a small market town for freshwater fish to a major center for the processing of crawfish.

CRAWFISH PONDS

Crawfish are hardy creatures that thrive best in wet, muddy areas. Usually they are found in ponds, ditches, streams, or rivers, where they often burrow underground for varying periods of time. Because they thrive in standing water and are scavengers that will eat practically anything, crawfish can be cultivated in artificial swamps or in other kinds of fields. Most of the research on crawfish cultivation has been performed in south Louisiana, which is now the world leader in crawfish production.

There are several types of crawfish farms, suited to differing environmental and economic circumstances. For example, crawfish flourish in rice fields after the rice has been harvested: the fields are flooded and "seeded" with crawfish, which eat the debris from the rice harvest and in turn fertilize the soil for the next rice crop. This method of raising crawfish is common in areas of southwest Louisiana where rice farms dominate the economy. Today large numbers of Louisiana rice farmers raise a summer crop of rice and a winter crop of crawfish.

In the Henderson area, where there is little rice production, crawfish are raised in artificial ponds. These ponds can be as large as two thousand acres and all are at least several hundred acres large. The ponds are constructed to simulate swamp conditions. To someone who doesn't know they are artificial, these ponds can be easily mistaken for true swampland. The principal difference is that the water in the artificial ponds can stagnate, and in order for the crawfish to breathe oxygen must be pumped in. In addition, the artificial ponds are drained during the summer to allow the vegetation to regrow, to eliminate predators, and to permit the crawfish that remain to burrow underground and survive the summer (La Caze 1976:15).

Because much of the area around Henderson was swamp initially, it has been relatively easy to convert it to crawfish ponds. By 1970 most of the area just south of Henderson, bordering on the natural Atchafalaya swamp, had been converted to crawfish ponds. In 1982 St. Martin Parish contained nearly 20,000 acres of crawfish ponds, mostly in the Henderson area.

Crawfish ponds can be exploited in several different ways. The usual pattern is for a landowner or an investor to convert a section of land to crawfish production, for personal use and for investment purposes. Often pond owners fish in their own ponds, but most of the fishing is done by others to whom fishing rights are leased in a kind of sharecropping system. Crawfish pond owners can net substantial profits if their ponds are adequately exploited, and many large landowners find this a satisfying way to use otherwise empty land.

Octave McGee is a retired sugar cane farmer who lives just outside the Henderson corporate limits. He still owns most of the land he used to farm, leasing it to others to work. He also has much undeveloped land, some of which he and a partner have converted to a small crawfish pond. They constructed artificial levees around the designated area, installed a pump system, flooded the land with water from a nearby canal, and stocked the pond with crawfish. They lease fishing rights to local fishers for one-third of the profits. They and their families also use the pond, and usually McGee can fill his freezer and those of his children with a year's supply of crawfish. If they wished to, they could earn more by having more fishers work it and by consuming less of the catch for themselves. For McGee, leasing his fishing rights is a way to make up the costs of catching his own crawfish, giving him a virtually free supply as well as a small additional income.

Not all pond owners own the land on which their ponds are located. Much of the land near Henderson is owned by a large holding company that leases land to interested area residents for various purposes. Buck Wyatt owns a crawfish pond together with his cousin Harvey. They lease the land on which the pond is located from this holding company, but they own the pumping system and all of the commercial rights to the pond. Their pond is a business enterprise, and they lease fishing rights to as many fishers as the pond will support. They also fish in it themselves. They use their pond as an investment and to make a living rather than for personal purposes.

Most owners of crawfish ponds have other sources of income besides the pond. Crawfish ponds can be highly profitable, but they are unpredictable because conditions are determined by the weather. McGee has income from his farm and from other investments, and Wyatt has a retirement pension from a job with a large company in a nearby city, as well as several other business ventures. These men derive secondary incomes from their ponds and agree that the pond is too unpredictable to use as a primary way to make a living.

Crawfish ponds are ordinarily seeded in late spring with the expectation that they will begin to produce in October. Because variables such as water temperature and depth can be controlled in a pond, it is possible to ensure that at least some fresh crawfish will be available at that time. Ponds can produce through late spring, but when wild crawfish (locally known as "deepwater" crawfish) become available in January or February, fishers stop working the ponds to avoid having to pay for fishing rights. Pond owners like Octave McGee may continue to work their ponds as late as they can, sometimes into the month of June, because they have no added expenses. As a result, pond crawfish generally predominate from October until midwinter when the deepwater crawfish become available, after which the swamp variety comprises the bulk of the crop.

Generally, deepwater crawfish are preferred over pond crawfish. They are usually larger and therefore easier and more worthwhile to peel. Professional crawfish peelers complain about small pond crawfish because they can make more money from larger animals. Some area residents claim that deepwater crawfish taste better; however, many cannot really tell the difference. Although they suffer from a less than favored reputation, pond crawfish differ from the wild ones mostly in size and are used successfully in all of the ways that deepwater ones are. Indeed, were it not for the crawfish ponds that have converted crawfishing into a year-round industry, the success of the industry would not be nearly as great as it is.

THE CRAWFISH INDUSTRY

It is almost impossible to estimate the full economic impact of the crawfish industry in Henderson. Much of the industry operates on a cash basis, and not all participants are careful about keeping records of earnings and/or payments. Some people participate in this industry precisely because it operates on a cash basis and there is no reliable way to ascertain the value of their earnings. The nature of the industry is such that people can work as much or as little as they want virtually whenever they want, picking up extra cash when they need it and quitting until they need money again. Probably most of the households in Henderson are in one way or another dependent on crawfish for at least part of their incomes, but more precise figures are not available.

The crawfish industry has directly produced several different types of jobs, and there are many more in other related enterprises such as restaurant work. Processing crawfish requires people to boil, weigh, package, and ship as well as to fish and peel. Most of the people who work with crawfish are either fishers or peelers. These occupations employ hundreds of Henderson area residents for all or part of the year.

In principle, fishers and processors are bound by an unwritten contract designed to protect the interests of both. A processor will agree to buy whatever a given fisher brings in, in return for which the fisher is expected to sell only to that one processor. Theoretically, this system guarantees the fisher a buyer and ensures a regular supply for the processor. This is a common system employed by fishers and fish dealers throughout the world, popular because it protects the interests of both (Acheson 1981:283). In Henderson this system is generally honored, but all parties are aware of violations on both sides. During peak season, when supply is high and prices low, fishers may find it more profitable to sell their catch at the roadside for retail prices than to the processor for wholesale. The plant owners complain that this is unfair competition for them because it reduces their supply and therefore their profits, and also because many customers prefer to buy direct from the fisher. In turn, when supply is so high that a plant cannot keep up with processing all that is brought in, the plant owner may inform the fishers that he will buy only three days a week. This can hurt the fishers, who may need the extra guaranteed income they get when they have a ready buyer for all of their catch. There is, then, some degree of flexibility on both sides despite the usual honoring of the contracts.

Technically, fishers are self-employed and are not on the regular payroll of the processing plants. They are independent, are not organized into a union or other trade organization, and have no fringe benefits or income security. They consider themselves to be contract laborers who sell a service and they expect immediate payment for what they provide. As a result, fishers are paid in cash as soon as they bring in their catch. Although they usually honor the agreements they have with the plant owners, fishers prefer not to be beholden to any particular plant owner. Immediate payment gives them a certain independence from the plant owners, which they enjoy. Also, fishing requires considerable temporary cash outlays for bait, and fishers want to recover their expenses as quickly as possible. Plant owners sometimes complain that this practice hurts them because they have to pay for the fish before they have a chance to sell it, and it leaves them short of cash. However, plant owners recognize that they would lose their fishers altogether if they were to change their method of payment, and so they accommodate the fishers as best they can.

Many fishers are fully dependent on fishing for their living, while others fish to supplement their incomes. Some fishers, such as Hector Landry, work seasonally at other jobs but quit to fish full time during crawfish season. Others fish on their days off, or during periods of occasional unemployment. Because it requires little long-term capital investment, crawfishing can be pursued with as much vigor as an individual chooses to invest.

Relations between the fishers and the plant owners are sometimes strained. Fishers tend to go out only when they want to and rarely notify the plant owner of their plans. As a result, the plant owners complain that they never know how many fishers are out on any given day and they have no way to predict how much peeling labor they will need nor how many orders they will be able to fill. For their part, the fishers complain that the plant owners control the price and that the fishers have no power in the industry they serve.

Processors do indeed control the price of crawfish, although the fishers can exercise some control over the supply and therefore indirectly influence the price. Early in the season, when supply is low, the price paid to the fisher is generally high, sometimes as much as 70 cents per pound. Early prices must be high in order to induce the fishers to go out for the low catch. However, as the season progresses and supply increases, prices drop considerably, sometimes to as low as 20 cents per pound. The processors can then take a higher markup on the final product and make more money because of volume sales to large customers who buy more because the price is low. When the price drops to a level that the fishers consider unsatisfactory, many discontinue fishing in the hopes that the price will go up again. Many fishers complain that when the season is too good they can't make any money because the price is too low. A fisher can stop working in the hopes that the price will rise, but if he depends on fishing for his living he will have to go out no matter what the price.

Traditionally, fishers have been relatively powerless to influence the nature of the market. However, in the spring of 1984 deepwater crawfishers staged a strike to protest low prices. The strike was organized by a local fisher who has worked as a college instructor and a professional photographer and who fishes to raise extra money. Participating fishers stayed home for a week, after which they settled with the processors for a guarantee of a minimum payment of 35 cents per pound (what the fishers claim is their break-even price) in return for a more consistently good product. This settlement was violated almost immediately, however, because some processors boycotted the fishers who had struck and some fishers agreed to sell for less than 35 cents. At this writing, the group of fishers is preparing to organize a processing cooperative that would give fishers complete control over their product, but final arrangements are not yet complete.

Although some of the plants in Henderson process crabs as well as crawfish, there are no crabs in the waters adjacent to Henderson. Crabs are saltwater animals and crabbers generally live closer to the coast. The crab processors in Henderson buy their crabs from coastal fishers, sometimes through middleman agents. Thus although crabs contribute considerably to the fishing economy in the Henderson area, they do not directly involve the fishers themselves.

Crawfishing is relatively simple, involving minimal equipment and no danger. In the swamps and ponds, crawfish are most commonly caught in traps that resemble small cages made of chicken wire. These traps are baited and set on poles in the water. After a couple of days the traps are lifted, the crawfish emptied into a sack, and fresh bait provided. In peak season one trap may contain 25 crawfish or more. All that is needed for crawfishing is a small skiff to haul the crawfish and to travel from one trap to another; the traps themselves; and sometimes a larger motor boat to travel to the location of the traps.

Crawfish traps are set and then abandoned in what are essentially public places. Ponds are fished by a restricted number of people, but any one of the fishers can gain access to another's traps. If there are no regular fishers in the pond, there is

A crawfish pond just outside of Henderson. Each of the poles supports a crawfish trap similar to the one in left foreground.

no way to prevent an unauthorized fisher from entering and emptying someone else's traps. This problem is compounded in the swamps, where anybody with a boat can fish at any time. There are occasional reports of crawfish theft and sometimes of theft of equipment left unattended near fishing grounds. The consensus of professional fishers is that only amateur fishers or professional thieves would steal someone else's crawfish. Indeed, reports of crawfish theft increased in 1983 when unemployment in the Henderson area was at a peak and many people began crawfishing to make up for lost jobs. Professional fishers maintain an honor system and do not poach on one another's traps, either in ponds or in the swamps. They emphasize that they are all in the same situation and are obligated to recognize one anothers' needs and property. There are never reports of conflicts or of accusations of theft among professional fishers, who know that for any of them to survive they must protect each others' interests.

Because it is so simple and requires so little investment, crawfishing is often a solitary occupation. Most fishers walk from one trap to the next, and the work can easily be performed by one person. Crawfishers sometimes work in pairs, usually pairs of relatives, but often this is for reasons of companionship rather than necessity. A few fishers have begun to work as pairs in a system that is quicker and more efficient than the older way of walking. Buck Wyatt and his wife have a motorized skiff in which they travel from trap to trap. Mrs. Wyatt raises and empties the traps and Mr. Wyatt rebaits the traps and replaces them in the water. This method

Noah Serrette raising a crawfish trap. The crawfish will be emptied into the container at the front of the boat.

is up to three or four times faster than the traditional method, but it requires teamwork and is most often performed by pairs of relatives. In either case, there is never any need for more than two people to crawfish together.

Fishers in the Henderson area are exclusively white and most of them are men. For a variety of reasons, local blacks and Vietnamese do not fish commercially, although many fish for recreation and for their own private consumption. There are a few women who fish commercially, most with their husbands, but a few independently. Mrs. Wyatt fishes with her husband but never by herself. Irma Davis is a middle-aged woman who now works as a peeler but used to fish commercially with her husband. Her sons now all work as commercial fishers. She was forced to stop fishing several years ago as a result of a heart attack, but she would prefer to fish if she could because

> when you're a fisherman you're your own boss, nobody tells you what to do or when to come to work. Also you make more money as a fisherman. But mostly you have the freedom to do whatever you want.

Charlotte Robin is in her mid-twenties. Her husband works irregular hours for an oil company, and when he is working she and her father, Hector Landry, fish together in a local pond. Much of what they catch they keep for themselves, but they also sell to a plant in the area. Charlotte has never held a regular job other than fishing because

> I think a wife should be home when she needs to be. That's why I like to do this. I can fish when I want, but if I have to stay home or I just want to stay home I can. I hate to do housework, though, and I never stay home just for that. I'd rather fish than anything else.

Irma and Charlotte are unusual in their preference for fishing. Although there appears to be no resistance to the idea of women fishing commercially, few women do, and those who do generally fish with men. Fishing is considered to be men's work, despite the fact that there is no danger and minimal physical strength required. Women's participation in the crawfish industry is concentrated in another task, that of peeling.

The purpose of fish processing is to produce edible meat in a form that is ready to cook. For crawfish and for crabs, this means peeling the meat out of the shell. Although several attempts have been made to create mechanical devices to peel crawfish and crabs, none of these attempts has been fully successful. As a result, all peeling must be performed by hand, and this labor employs large numbers of people in Henderson and the surrounding area. The techniques for peeling crawfish and crabs are similar, though there are minor differences resulting from the differ-

Peeling crawfish at one of Henderson's larger crawfish plants. At periodic intervals the colander will be weighed and emptied, and the peeler will begin again.

ences in the anatomy of the animals. A plant can easily accommodate both craw-fish and crabs without any modification, and any worker can easily peel either.

Until recently, all crawfish peelers were women. Today there are a few young men working as peelers. Most of these men are Vietnamese, though a few are Cajuns. However, the overwhelming majority of peelers are still women—black, white, and Vietnamese—and at least one local plant owner refers to his peelers as "the ladies."

Like the fishers, peelers are paid in cash according to how much they produce rather than by the hour. As of this writing, the going rate is 90 cents per pound of peeled meat. Peelers are also considered to be self-employed contract laborers, and like the fishers they work whenever they choose. Unlike the fishers, however, peelers do not have the kind of informal contract binding them to a single plant. The lack of this kind of arrangement works to the benefit of both peelers and plant owners. Because the fish supply is unpredictable, during slack seasons some of the smaller plants may not be able to remain open every day. During peak season the plants may have to be open longer hours to keep up with the supply. Many peelers are on the roster of more than one plant, so that if one is closed they can report to work at another. Some do not like to peel crabs, which take longer and are more difficult to peel than crawfish; these workers may report to a plant that is peeling crawfish on a day when their usual place of work is peeling crabs.

As a result of this flexibility, it is difficult to estimate the number of people employed as peelers. A count of available names at all of the plants will contain a great deal of duplication because many peelers work at more than one plant. Peltier's, the largest crawfish plant in Henderson, has between 70 and 100 peelers on the roster, but they are never all there at once. On any given day there may be only 50 peelers working at Peltier's, and from 12 to 35 at the smaller plants. It is safe to say that several hundred people are employed as peelers at least part time.

Peeling crawfish or crabs is monotonous work that requires little concentration or skill. Some women have been working as peelers for as long as 25 years. In order for this kind of work to be tolerable, many work in teams of friends or relatives. Groups of friends will work at the same plant, where they can pass the time in conversation. Virginia Dupuis, a woman in her fifties, explained that she works as a peeler because otherwise she'd just sit around the house and talk with her friends; this way she can earn some money while she talks with her friends. Most peelers depend on the income more than does Mrs. Dupuis, but there is no question that the work is made more pleasant by having friends or relatives with whom to share it.

The flexibility of the peeling operation makes it possible for peelers to arrange all sorts of financial and social strategies to make their work easier. A peeler can bring in a friend to work for one day. The visitor can be placed on the payroll or, more commonly, can peel into the "pot" of the friend and the two can make their own arrangements concerning the division of the proceeds. At Peltier's, several of the regular peelers are neighbors in a rural community about 15 miles from Henderson. Not all have access to cars, so they have arranged a car pool. One day a week all of the passengers peel in the name of the owner of the car, giving her their income for that day. This constitutes their payment for the use of her car. In general, plant owners are indifferent to the complex financial arrangements of their employees; as long as the work gets done, it makes no difference to them who gets paid for it.

Because of the nature of the work, peeling attracts workers from well beyond the immediate area of Henderson. In fact, Henderson alone is not big enough to supply all of its own peeling needs. Some of the larger plants bring in labor from communities as much as 30 miles away, and at least two provide free bus service for their employees. The economic impact of the crawfish industry therefore is felt well beyond the limits of the town of Henderson.

The crawfish industry has created jobs besides fishing and peeling, and it has spawned support services such as the making of crawfish traps and the selling of chicken wire, rubber hip boots, and bait. It has also contributed substantially to Henderson's emergence as a restaurant center. As a result, the crawfish industry in one way or another affects virtually every household in Henderson and many others over a wide surrounding area. When asked what Henderson would be like if there were no crawfish industry, one lifelong resident replied,

Oh, Lord, I can't even imagine. I guess there wouldn't be much. You just can't think about Henderson without crawfish. It just doesn't make any sense.

4 / Restaurants

Although crawfish dominates the economy of Henderson and the everyday lives of many of its residents, the restaurants comprise another major source of revenue and employment. Henderson's restaurants are well known and popular with residents from all over Louisiana, who may travel several hours strictly to eat there. Henderson's restaurants have been publicized in major newspapers such as the *New York Times* and in several books about U.S. food. As a result, out-of-state visitors arrive looking to eat at one of the restaurants for which the town is known.

THE RESTAURANTS

At this writing, Henderson has 12 eating establishments and one lunch counter built into another business. In addition, there are three or four restaurants located immediately outside the corporate limits of the town. These establishments range from fast-food fried chicken and take-out sandwich shops to sit-down restaurants with white tablecloths, linen napkins, and wine lists. There is a continuum from restaurants catering exclusively to locals to those oriented toward visitors. Some, such as the fried chicken and take-out joints, are strictly local in appeal, but most have mixed clientele and their menus and atmospheres reflect this diversity.

Excluding the fast-food establishments, which are relatively new, all of Henderson's restaurants feature local fish and seafood cuisine. (Cajuns, including those in the Henderson area, also specialize in meat and game cooking. However, these are domestic foods, not generally served in restaurants. Those restaurants that do feature this kind of cooking are locally oriented and do not advertise this aspect of their menus.) Although some restaurants have larger and more diverse menus than others, most of the menus are similar and almost all feature crawfish as house specialties. A typical menu includes several preparations of crawfish, crabs, and shrimp, fried catfish, and other varieties of fish cooked in different ways. Most of the restaurants feature at least some relatively fancy or elaborate dishes, and all have a complement of simpler ones as well. Some serve sandwiches while others concentrate exclusively on higher priced full meals. Some serve

31

boiled seafood—popular with locals but messy to serve and to eat—while others do not. Some are busiest at lunchtime, while others do most of their trade in the evenings. Identical menu items are quite similar in style and quality at most establishments—fried catfish at one tastes much like fried catfish at another—but each restaurant has its own specialties.

RESTAURANT CLIENTELE

Henderson residents and those from the surrounding area make regular use of these restaurants. Some restaurants serve as hangouts for the friends of the owner, where people can buy a beer or a cup of coffee and sit with friends for a couple of hours. Others are more formal and are patronized by groups of family and friends eating together and only rarely by individuals looking for friends. The more casual restaurants generally do a larger local lunchtime trade, while the others are patronized even by locals in the evenings. Even the most elaborate of these restaurants is locally owned and all feature local cuisine that resembles Henderson home cooking. As a result, when local residents eat there they do so as a matter of convenience or for a change of scenery rather than to eat something out of the ordinary.

In general, residents prefer the informal atmosphere of the locally oriented restaurants. The formal table settings of the tourist restaurants are not familiar to most Cajuns, who tend to be casual about everything they do and are uncomfortable with formality on every level. In addition, many women, especially middle aged and over, feel that it is their responsibility to feed their families. They are unaccustomed to being served by others, especially by strangers. However, residents frequently order out from the tourist establishments, particularly if they live next door or if the restaurant has a specialty they like. Virginia Dupuis often orders seafood platters (combination plates of fried seafood including shrimp, crawfish, crabmeat, frog legs, and other items) from Broussard's, but she orders them to go and she and her family eat them at home. She explains that it's too expensive to eat out because of the extra costs of drinks, coffee, and the tip. However, as less expensive restaurants with similar seafood platters are available down the street, it is likely that she simply feels uncomfortable eating in an environment in which she is served by someone else.

What determines whether a restaurant appeals to locals or to tourists is a combination of atmosphere, diversity of menu, cooking style, price, and the personality of the proprietor. Pat's Waterfront Restaurant, for example, is relatively fancy and expensive and is predominantly a tourist establishment. It is the oldest extant restaurant in Henderson and the most famous. It was built during the 1950s, adjacent to the original Guidry's Place, which was subsequently torn down to make a parking lot for Pat's. Now owned by Agnes Huval, the ex-wife of the original owner and the town's mayor, Pat's Waterfront attracts more out-of-town visitors than any other Henderson restaurant. This is largely because it advertises most heavily and has an established reputation and a scenic view. Tourists are the main clientele here, and Agnes does her best to attract them. She says that tourists are what make this place what it is. Henderson would be nothing without the tourists. I want to have my place look nice for the people who keep me in business.

Nonetheless, although Pat's main clientele is tourists, it does a sizable local trade as well. The local customers range from friends of the owner to townspeople there for a nice lunch. The popularity of Pat's with local customers derives in part from Agnes's willingness to accommodate local citizens, serving them smaller portions of menu items on request, or items not on the menu at all. Friends of the owner will go to the kitchen for their own coffee, sit at a table, and wait for someone to have time for a chat. Robert Theriot regularly visits, helps himself to what he wants, stays for a while to see his friends, and leaves when the restaurant gets too busy. It is common for Agnes, her family, and a few friends to be seated over coffee and hamburgers in a separate section of the dining room while tourists eat seafood platters a few feet away.

In contrast, Broussard's restaurant down the road from Pat's does much less local business. This restaurant is also geared primarily toward outsiders, and like Pat's it features white tablecloths, linen napkins, and relatively high prices. The menu is more varied than that at Pat's, but the style and quality of the food at the two establishments are very similar. Yet Broussard's has fewer local customers because all customers are treated alike there. Friends of the owner are not greeted and seated in a separate corner of the dining room, as they are at Pat's, and they do not have the option of ordering off the menu. There is rarely a collection of local residents chatting over coffee in the dining room. Local residents eat there when they want a large, formal meal, but they do not consider it a place to go to pass the time. Instead Broussard's thrives on a busy tourist trade and on banquets, for which they have good facilities.

Pat Huval has opened up two new restaurants in Henderson since Agnes took control of the Waterfront. One of these is located directly across the canal from the Waterfront, and by taking advantage of the same scenic view it provides direct competition for the older establishment. However, at this writing the original Waterfront remains more popular. Of Pat's two new restaurants, his locally oriented one is by far the more successful. The front room was designed as a bar, short-order counter, and poolroom, with the dining room off to the side behind doors that are usually closed. The design effectively restricted the clientele to locals as visitors were discouraged by the poolroom and the fact that they could not see the dining room. Subsequently the pool tables were replaced by dining tables and tourist trade picked up. But the decor remained more locally oriented, with simple tables covered with oilcloths and no formal seating. In addition, the simple menu features items more of interest to locals: it has a variety of sandwiches and several blue-plate luncheon specials that vary from day to day. The intent behind this restaurant was to provide local people with a place to eat at moderate prices in an informal atmosphere. Pat describes this as a "working man's restaurant" and says that he kept it simple

> because it got so people who lived here couldn't hardly find a place to eat. Every-thing was too expensive. So I gave them a place with simple food at good prices, where they feel like they can come whenever they want.

Tourists are welcome, of course, but they are not the *raison d'être* of this establishment.*

Local friendships and rivalries can also determine who visits which restaurants. Pat's Waterfront has customers from the Henderson area and from Breaux Bridge, but some residents of nearby Cecilia prefer not to eat there. They are more allied with the Broussard family, some of whom live in Cecilia, and with one of the other restaurant owners who also lives in Cecilia. In addition, because Pat Huval is a highly controversial local figure (a point discussed in Chapter 7), many Henderson residents dislike him and will not patronize his restaurants. These feelings can be so strong that one resident refused an invitation to a party because she thought it was to be held at one of Pat's restaurants; when she learned otherwise, she agreed to attend.

Cajun cuisine is generally highly seasoned. Some of the tourist-oriented establishments make special efforts to tone down the seasoning to appeal to outsiders not accustomed to the Cajun penchant for cayenne pepper. The manager of Broussard's has stated that he seasons his food differently from most area restaurants and that outsiders prefer it that way. However, although some restaurants appeal more to tourists than others, virtually all see some tourist business. Most visitors prefer the more refined atmospheres and formal service of the tourist-oriented establishments, but a few enjoy the simplicity and lower prices of the local ones. As a result, all of the restaurants in the area serve food that differs in some degree from home cooking, which is usually even spicier that that served at the most locally oriented restaurants. The residents generally agree that the best cooking in the Henderson area is not to be found in the restaurants at all, but rather in the homes, where people season their food to their own tastes without regard for the cash register.

THE RESTAURANT BUSINESS

Operating a restaurant anywhere takes considerable capital, business sense, and, ideally, experience, as well as a favorable economy. Most of the more successful restaurants in Henderson are owned by people who have worked in the food service business for many years. A few of the restauranteurs originally worked for Pat Huval when he first had the Waterfront and were trained by him before opening their own places. This is especially true for the most tourist-oriented establishments: one of these is operated by Pat himself, one by his ex-wife Agnes, one by Pat's brother, and another by a nonrelative who worked for Pat at the Waterfront for several years. Most of the locally oriented restaurants began as small, informal eating places with minimal investment in equipment and fixtures, and have expanded with their business. Some restaurants are owned by people who at one time or another owned nightclubs: Fernand Broussard, owner of the old

---

* This restaurant was closed when Pat merged his businesses in the summer of 1984. The staff and much of the clientele moved to the newly consolidated restaurant, which used the same advertising campaign: a place where people can afford to eat out again.

Moonlight Club, now owns a restaurant (operated by his son), and Pat himself began in the nightclub business. The restaurant industry breeds its own successes and futures, and it is difficult for a place to survive if the proprietor has not been in the business for a while.

As a result, there is a certain amount of instability and uncertainty in the restaurant business. The early 1980s were characterized by an economic slowdown in Henderson as in the rest of the United States, and the restaurants were particularly hard hit. The oil industry, which had at one time provided generous expense accounts that permitted executives to eat in Henderson frequently, slowed down and cut back on these benefits. Many Henderson area residents lost their oil-related jobs and were unable to patronize the restaurants as much as they had previously. A few restaurants had trouble meeting their expenses; those owned by less experienced people were hit especially badly. During the four years I worked in Henderson, one restaurant changed ownership four times and was still unable to succeed. (Toward the end of my stay it reopened under a fifth ownership.) In addition, a pizzeria opened and closed and an established local fish restaurant went out of business after its owner died. (It was subsequently re-opened by another owner.) In all cases of restaurant failure, the proprietors had limited restaurant experience: the pizzeria was opened by a young couple just out of school; the restaurant that changed hands so many times passed from a bar owner to several investors to some young couples also just out of school; and the fish house passed to the owner's widow, who did not know enough about the business to keep it running.

The restaurants that closed were all locally oriented. It may be that the economic situation in Henderson during this period contributed to the decline of these establishments. Business was slow in the tourist places as well, but in spite of their higher overhead expenses, none of these places closed. All of the tourist restaurants are operated by highly experienced restauranteurs who were able to make the best of bad times. Young people with little experience and small amounts of capital are likely to open a more modest establishment, which appears to be the kind most likely to fail. In a very real sense, then, the restaurant business in Henderson is a tourist-oriented business.

RESTAURANTS AND TOURISTS

Almost all of Henderson's restaurants are willing and eager to take advantage of the tourist trade. Even the ones that don't cater explicitly to outsiders sell souvenirs to the occasional visitor who may stop in. Records of Cajun music are especially popular, and most Henderson restaurants have large displays containing a wide selection of these records. Other items sold include cookbooks and handicrafts. Most of these are sold on a consignment basis, so they entail no expense to the restaurants and provide small additional sources of revenue.

In addition to selling souvenirs, the restaurants that cater to outsiders also provide other services to their customers that the locally oriented ones do not. These places informally interpret Cajun culture and history to their visitors, many of whom are unfamiliar with it. Some restaurants have paper placemats (sometimes placed over the white tablecloths) that recount the history of the Cajuns. Waitresses good-naturedly explain to bewildered customers the proper way to eat boiled crawfish. They also answer questions about Cajun life.

Besides being spicier than the norm in other parts of the United States, Cajun cuisine includes some "exotic" ingredients. This is especially true in Henderson where the restaurants are organized around crawfish cuisine, virtually unavailable elsewhere in this country (except in parts of Texas, where large numbers of Cajuns now live). At those restaurants oriented toward tourists, the food tends to be less heavily spiced than at the local places. These establishments feature some local items in forms more familiar to non-Cajuns, such as crawfish or crab-meat salads and steaks.

One of the waitresses at Pat's has been working there since the restaurant opened 30 years ago. She enjoys her interactions with the tourists because

> you meet people from all over. I learn a lot here talking to all those people. They like to hear about us, you know, the Cajuns, and I like to hear about them. It's more fun when you get to talk to people from all over.

Part of this woman's job, as both she and her employer perceive it, is to make the visitors feel welcome and to explain to them anything they need explained.

In contrast, the locally oriented restaurants generally do little to accommodate the special needs of outsiders. These establishments use heavier amounts of pepper in their food and the menus do not contain printed descriptions of the Cajun dishes that are unknown in other places. French is frequently the dominant language at these establishments, although all but the very oldest residents of Henderson can speak English. Although they are not designed with the intent of keeping tourists away, some outsiders feel uncomfortable in an environment in which little English is to be heard and where most of the food is unfamiliar.

As a result of the contrast between local and tourist restaurants, visitors who come to Henderson to eat may get a distorted view of the community. If their experiences are limited to eating at one of the tourist-oriented restaurants, they will see formal service, relatively high prices, toned-down seasonings, and be met by an English-speaking staff. Yet among themselves, Henderson residents are casual, economical, and speak French in most personal and intimate contexts. In a very important way, the restaurants protect the privacy of local residents while per-mitting them to share something of themselves and their culture with visitors. This is important, and it is a point to which I will return.

RESTAURANTS AND THE ECONOMY

The economic impact of Henderson's restaurants is more variable than is that of the crawfish industry. Crawfish are a popular dietary item among south Louisianians, and the demand for them is relatively constant both locally and from the com-mercial buyers around the country. In contrast, eating in restaurants is a luxury that can be cut from a budget when money is tight. Many of Henderson's restaurant patrons are vacationers, and long vacations are also dispensable luxuries. In good times, when the restaurants are crowded, they generate a lot of money and employ several hundred people. During the economic slowdown of the early 1980s, many people were laid off from their restaurant jobs, and even the most successful restaurants suffered diminished business.

During peak seasons Pat's Waterfront alone may employ over 50 people as waitresses, cooks, bus help, hostesses, and office workers. The other tourist restaurants may employ up to 30 apiece, and the locally oriented establishments employ numbers ranging from a handful to 15 or 20. Wages at the restaurants are not high, but when the economy is good a waitress at one of the tourist restaurants can make a great deal in tips. Kitchen workers do not have the added income from tips and so their incomes are generally lower.

Most of the restaurant workers are women. None of the restaurants in Henderson employs men to wait on tables, and the waitress staffs comprise the largest proportion of employees at all of these establishments. Cooks are almost always women as well. Most of the restaurants are owned by men or have men working in office or management positions. In addition, men may work as janitors, bartenders, and bus help. But because there are fewer of these positions, men comprise a minority of restaurant employees.

Waiting on tables is difficult work but many consider it more desirable than peeling crawfish, the other local alternative for women with limited formal educations. Waitressing and peeling crawfish can both yield sizable earnings for a worker depending on performance. However, waitressing is more dependable (given a good economy) because there are no off-seasons as there are in the crawfish industry. Also, waiting tables is considered "cleaner" work, more suitable for younger women, and the physical conditions are better. Peeling crawfish "messes up your hands," as one veteran peeler put it, and so young women prefer other work. Of course, there is a tradeoff: waitresses must report to work when expected and they have less control over their schedules than do crawfish peelers. Because there are fewer waitress jobs than peeling jobs, waitresses cannot drop in and out of the workforce as easily as peelers can.

All of Henderson's restaurants are locally owned and managed and are run as small family businesses. As a result, it is common to find that large numbers of employees at a restaurant are related to the owner. Pat's Waterfront employs the owner's son, three sisters, and a nephew. Pat Huval's tourist restaurant was originally managed by his nephew and subsequently by his son. Pat's wife manages the local restaurant with assistance from her mother and her children. Broussard's is owned by Fernand Broussard, managed by his son, and also employs his daughter. Given the large and extended nature of families in Henderson, the tendency to hire relatives is not necessarily a liability; most residents are at least distantly related to somebody in the restaurant business. Because family members are the last to lose their jobs during recessionary times, it sometimes appears that nobody but relatives works at these restaurants. This is not the case; all hire from outside their families when they need the extra help. A restaurant that employs 30 waitresses must of necessity hire nonrelatives. Nonetheless, restaurant jobs are not as openly available as crawfish-peeling jobs, particularly when business is slow.

Because there are so many of them, the restaurants collectively contribute a large portion of the Henderson town budget. According to the mayor, in 1983 the restaurants provided roughly 20 percent of the town's revenues; this figure would be considerably higher during better economic times. (There is also some concern locally that some of the restaurants do not report their sales tax earnings accurately.) This, however, is not a wholly accurate assessment of the financial contribution of the restaurants. Because so many restaurant patrons are not from the area, the money generated in sales taxes is largely outside money. Other businesses in town simply redistribute local money, while the restaurants provide new sources of funds. (The crawfish industry, which also caters largely to outsiders, contributes relatively less in sales taxes because most of the major customers are commercial firms, which buy at wholesale prices and therefore pay less in sales taxes. Retail customers of the crawfish plants are, generally speaking, from Henderson or the surrounding area.) The restaurants also permit Henderson to receive funds from the state alcohol tax, funds that are allocated in proportion to the amount of liquor sold. In a very important sense, then, the economic base of the town depends heavily on the restaurants.

The emergence of Henderson as a restaurant capital was largely a product of the development of the crawfish industry, and the restaurants still depend on the local crawfish industry for their success. Henderson actually derives more of its identity and income for its residents from the crawfish industry. The restaurants, however, have made Henderson famous across Louisiana and elsewhere, and they are important economically and socially to the life of the town. Crawfish may come first, but the restaurants are indispensable to the community.

5/Family life, sex roles, and the perpetuation of Cajun culture

Cajuns have long been known for their close-knit families. Traditionally, rural Cajun families were large—12 children was not an uncommon size—and were characterized by considerable intermarriage among cousins. Most early Cajun communities were composed of collections of relatives living on adjacent pieces of property, and the communities developed as local families grew. As a result, it was difficult for nonrelatives to meet and marriages were frequently made between cousins of varying degrees (first-cousin marriages are illegal in Louisiana but were sometimes performed anyway; more distant cousins can marry with no difficulty). Cousin marriage also had the advantage of keeping property within family groupings, and sometimes were preferred by parents for this reason. Because there has been a great deal of residential continuity over the generations in most Cajun communities, today it is understood in small towns that most residents are related to one another.

Henderson's history is somewhat unusual among Cajun communities because the town is relatively new and does not have residential continuity extending back two centuries. However, most of the original settlers were related when they arrived from Atchafalaya. In addition, the small farming community that has been incorporated into Henderson contained families that had been there for generations. There is, then, a great deal of interrelatedness even in Henderson, and it can appear to an outsider as though everybody is everybody else's cousin. I once expressed surprise when Denise LeBlanc, a Henderson native, told me she was related to someone else whom we were discussing. Denise's response to my surprise was surprise of her own. "Everybody in Henderson is related, didn't you know that?"

The interrelatedness of the community is compounded by the fact that in the recent past (and sometimes even today) pairs of siblings would marry: two brothers married two sisters, for example. There are at least two pairs of such couples in Henderson today. Robert Theriot and his brother married Usie sisters, and Buck Wyatt and his sister married a Prejean sister and brother. The children of these couples are double cousins, making kinship ties even more complicated and more firm than they would be ordinarily.

Surnames in the Henderson area are remarkably uniform. The Henderson telephone directory has four listings for Smith and none for Jones or Brown. But there are some four dozen Guidrys, almost 30 LeBlancs, and as many Latiolais, Patins, and Robins. People may therefore share a last name and be unrelated or so distantly related that nobody can calculate the degree. Under these circumstances it is possible for siblings to marry unrelated persons with the same last name. The husbands of sisters Wendy and Denise LeBlanc are unrelated, but because the sisters married men with the same last name it is sometimes assumed that their husbands are brothers. Last name in a town like Henderson is little indication of the degree of relatedness.

Whatever Denise LeBlanc claims, it is not true that everybody in Henderson is related. Even among the interrelated population, the term "cousin" can be applied to people who elsewhere in the United States would be classed as second, third, or even fourth cousins, degrees that are virtually meaningless. And there are several outsiders living in Henderson, people who have settled there because it provides them with country living in relatively close proximity to employment centers in Lafayette. Longtime residents sometimes complain that "You don't know everybody in town anymore." These newcomers, of course, are not part of the extensive cousin network of the community, although their children may eventually marry into it. In addition, the black and Vietnamese communities in Henderson are less interrelated than is the white population because they are smaller and because the Vietnamese community is so new. There is also little intermarriage among the racial groups, so few whites are closely related to either the blacks or the Vietnamese. However, because many of the outsiders participate little in community life and because the established white Cajuns are the majority of the population, popular opinion equates Henderson with the white Cajuns. Within this group, at least, most members are related to many others.

RESIDENCE PATTERNS AND HOUSEHOLD COMPOSITION

Today, as always, the ideal household in the Henderson area contains a nuclear family composed of two parents and their children. This, of course, is the model family in Western societies. In this respect Henderson is like most other communities in the United States. However, in Henderson the nuclear family is only half the story. There is a strong dependence on other relatives who live nearby, and there is sufficient variation in household composition that the classic nuclear family is less common than many residents suggest. Relationships among family members are strong, and in a community where "everybody is related," people have wide networks of kinship obligations and bonds that extend beyond their households and throughout the town and the surrounding area.

Cajuns generally feel strongly about taking care of their own relatives and are opposed to such institutions as nursing homes unless absolutely necessary. Several households in Henderson contain elderly parents and grandparents who can no longer care for themselves. This has created households that vary from the model nuclear family. The Melancon family, for example, is composed of three brothers and two sisters, all middle aged with grown children of their own. Their mother, old Mrs. Melancon, is alive but in failing health. All of the Melancon siblings have regular jobs and therefore have limited time but adequate incomes to place their mother in a home where she would receive the medical care and personal attention she requires. However, they have opted not to do this. Old Mrs. Melancon spends one month at a time with each of her children, moving from household to household. The siblings thereby share the costs and the burdens of caring for her. One of the sisters explained that

> we Cajuns just don't do things that way [use nursing homes] if we don't have to. The old people should be at home if they can. It's all right if you have no other way to take care of them, but we can take care of our mother ourselves and that's how it should be.

Each Melancon household is a nuclear family for most of the time, but for one month out of five each becomes an extended family household.

Another source of variation from the typical nuclear family derives from the Cajun pattern of having adult children remain in their parents' home until they marry. Traditionally, Cajuns married young and it was rare for an adult to be unmarried. Today, although Cajuns still marry young by U.S. standards, they usually wait until they are old enough to be financially independent of their parents. In urban areas of the United States, young single people with jobs take apartments away from their parents; in Henderson, as in the Cajun area generally, children and parents both consider this a waste of money. As a result, a household may contain several adult children, all with good jobs and independent incomes, living with their parents. At least one household in Henderson contains the elderly parents with one middle-aged bachelor son, who has lived with his parents for most of his life. In a strict sense this is a nuclear family, but elsewhere in the United States self-supporting adults would not live with their parents, and so the Henderson household is not entirely typical of the U.S. pattern.

Traditionally, Cajun mothers refused to attend the weddings of their children because they were "too sad" that their children were leaving home. Today Cajun mothers eagerly attend their childrens' weddings, although they remain sad that their children are leaving. This sadness is sometimes partly alleviated by postmarital residence patterns that keep a young couple close to one set of parents. Because Cajuns tend to marry young, few newlyweds can afford to buy a house. In the Henderson area, where ties to the land and to kin are very strong, most prefer not to move to a larger town where they might be able to rent an inexpensive apartment. Instead, many couples set up trailers on land borrowed, leased, or sometimes bought from one set of parents. There is no preference for residence with the husband's or the wife's family; the choice is made according to which side can provide the more favorable situation. Charlotte Robin lives with her husband in a trailer adjacent to her parents' house because they have more land than her husband's family does. In contrast, Wayne and Betty LeBlanc moved their trailer from a commercial trailer park to his parents' land when Betty became pregnant, in order to save the rent they had been paying for their lot. Often when a young couple lives on parental property the trailer becomes an extension of the parents' house, used for little more than sleeping and for an occasional meal. The lives of the young couple may be fully integrated with those of the parents on whose

House and trailer, a few miles outside of Henderson. The trailer is occupied by a married child of the owners of the house.

land they live, and the independence of the household may be more apparent than real.

In rare instances this pattern is carried to the even greater extreme of having the young couple live with one set of parents until they can become financially solvent. In a community near Henderson one household contains two married sons and their wives, in addition to the parents and other siblings. One of these couples has two young children. This is a rare and extreme occurrence and is possible only because the family in question is well-to-do and has a large house with room for privacy. However, other households in the Henderson area also sometimes include married children for varying lengths of time. One Henderson woman told me of her remorse that her eldest son was planning to marry within a few months. She consoled herself with the fact that

> it won't be like he's really getting married, though, because they're planning to live at home for a while. Probably six months to a year, until they can save themselves a *good* downpayment for a trailer.

This residence pattern can extend well into later life. Louise Theriot, who with her husband Robert is now retired, lives within a few houses of each of her three sisters. Bernard Dupuis's mother lives directly across the street from his house. Percy Serrette, a 35-year-old bachelor, lives next door to his parents.

In recent years another type of extended family household has become increasingly prevalent. For a wide variety of reasons, the rate of illegitimate births has been increasing dramatically throughout the area. Young women are no longer marrying as early as they once did, and changing mores have made premarital sex more acceptable than it was in the past. Even ten years ago couples routinely got married because of pregnancy; today this is less common. At least one local Catholic priest now discourages couples from marrying simply because of pregnancy on the grounds that such marriages frequently end in divorce and can cause more suffering to all parties than if they had never occurred at all. The result of these changes is that many single women still living with their parents are now having babies that formerly they would not have had or that would have caused them to marry. Although not typical, it is no longer unusual for a household in the Henderson area to contain parents, several grown but unmarried children, and the illegitimate child (sometimes children) of a daughter.

In general, Henderson residents express the standard U.S. norm preferring nuclear households and they claim that a couple should establish an independent residence at marriage. They also maintain that children should be raised in a separate household with their parents. Situations such as the ones discussed here—where couples live adjacent to or with one set of parents, or where a daughter lives with her parents and her child—are cited by residents as exceptions and as responses to financial need. However, such cases are more common than many residents maintain. These households demonstrate the strength of Cajun family ties, and they illustrate that in a context of strong family ties and close geographic proximity it may be difficult to distinguish between nuclear and extended family households.

KINSHIP OBLIGATIONS AND COOPERATION

Because of the close emotional and geographic ties among family members, Cajuns maintain extensive sets of obligations to their various relatives. The large size of Cajun families means that individuals may spend much of their time fulfilling obligations to one relative or another. These obligations are many and varied, ranging from assistance with major work tasks to help running errands and working in a family-owned business.

Traditionally, Cajuns were more dependent on kin cooperation than they are now. This is especially true for farmers, who may have limited time in which to plant and reap a crop and who previously did not have access to the equipment that now makes it possible to do much of the work alone. Before universal cash labor, when money was scarce, people helped each other in turns out of physical and economic necessity. Cooperative labor, involving groups of neighbors who were often also kin, was a fundamental part of traditional Cajun culture. Cajuns have a term, in French, for cooperative work: *coups de main* (literally "helping hand"). Today *coups de main* are less important both physically and economically than they once were, but they are still practiced and the term is still in use.

Most commonly, relatives help each other with work-related tasks such as construction, repairs, and other domestic chores. Usually this cooperation is among groups of men, but women trade off tasks like babysitting, and often a mother and her daughter will help each other with major housecleaning. One young woman told me that she sometimes takes her ironing to her sister's house, and while her sister irons the clothes she cleans her sister's kitchen. In a community adjacent to Henderson, a young couple wanted to add a carport to the side of their house. The husband called his relatives and one Saturday seven men together built the carport.

Because so many young women now have paying jobs, they are required to make babysitting arrangements for their children. There are quite a few nurseries and day-care centers in the Henderson area, but most women prefer to leave their children with relatives if at all possible. They say that "a stranger can't love your baby like you do," and, presumably, like other relatives will. As a result, many Henderson grandmothers do regular babysitting and child-care duty. As with postmarital residence, the babysitting grandmother can be either paternal or maternal. One mother from Henderson, who now lives in Lafayette, leaves her young child with her mother in Henderson despite the fact that she must drive several miles out of her way to do so. She says this is the only way she can be sure her child is properly cared for. Grandmothers generally enjoy taking care of their grandchildren and view it as an obligation they have to their families. Except under the most dire circumstances, no grandmother would refuse to babysit.

Cajuns take their sibling relationships very seriously, and it is among siblings that most labor is exchanged. Cousin relationships, in contrast, are invoked only selectively. This is essential in a community in which most people can claim to be cousins with most others. Cousins who like one another may use the fact of being cousins to reinforce an already strong personal tie, but those who do not get along can easily ignore the family tie. One Henderson native has long maintained a close friendship with his first cousin Harry. He introduces Harry as his cousin, and the two cooperate in many tasks and activities. However, this man has less regard for Harry's brother Charles, and he refers to Charles not as "my cousin" but as "Harry's brother." In other words, he acknowledges the kinship tie with Harry but not with Charles, and when referring to Charles he invokes Harry as a friend rather than as a relative. There is no expectation that he should cooperate with Charles as he does with Harry because the two do not get along.

Cooperation among relatives and the closeness of family ties have created work patterns in which siblings and sometimes cousins work together. One group of brothers owns a construction company; the restaurants, as I have discussed, are mostly family operations; and it is common for sisters or female cousins to peel crawfish together. Brothers, fathers and sons, or sometimes husbands and wives, fish together, and the office manager of one of the fish-processing plants is the sister of the owner. Wendy LeBlanc owns a beauty shop where her sister Denise is employed. Wendy and Denise both insist that they cannot imagine not working with a relative; working with "strangers" would be difficult because there could be unforeseen personality conflicts. Relatives help each other out anyway, and it is easier if they make the cooperative relationship official.

Because families have lived in the area sometimes for two centuries and certainly for many generations, reputations accrue to names, and a person may be marked by virtue of a surname. The Angelle family has been heavily involved in state-level politics for several generations, and some of its members are reputed to be unscrupulous. An Angelle is therefore assumed to be argumentative and not necessarily honest, and people will look for political or manipulative motives behind what an Angelle does. As in many rural communities, young people are identified by who their parents are. An older person, when meeting an unfamiliar younger person, will commonly ask "Who's your daddy?" as a means of identification.

However, although families have reputations and cooperative obligations are strong, siblings are not necessarily expected to join one another in personal rivalries. A heritage of age-old family feuds does not exist in the Henderson area, although some individuals do hold grudges for long periods of time. For several years the mayor, Pat Huval, has engaged in a bitter and public rivalry with the chief of police. The chief's brothers, however, are not expected to boycott the mayor's businesses or to involve themselves in any way in the arguments. As the mayor himself put it,

> I don't have nothing against those people. They're all good, hardworking people. But the chief and I just don't see things the same and I can't work with him. It's him, not the rest of them that I don't want to deal with.

Likewise, relatives are not expected to do business with one another if better deals can be made with outsiders. It is understood in Henderson that business is business, and people are not expected to give discounts or special consideration in business deals to their relatives. Donating time and effort to a major project in a family *coup de main* may be expected. Giving discounts in business is not expected because "everybody has to make a living." This practice is essential in a community where most people can claim at least a distant kinship tie with most others; if discounts were expected, nobody in Henderson would pay (or receive) full price for anything.

Kinship obligations are strong but selective, invoked in certain contexts but not in others. Reciprocal cooperation has always been important to people who lacked ready cash and who like to do things for themselves; in Henderson it is understood that people need help from kin to survive. However, kin are not expected to do one another's dirty work or to engage in rivalries on each other's behalf. Because families can be quite large, nobody is expected to be on equally good terms with all of their many cousins. In a town in which "everybody is related," kin obligations provide extensive networks that help people accomplish what they need but provide only limited constraints on an individual's freedom.

FAMILY CYCLE

Cajuns value children highly. One reason for the traditional large size of Cajun families is the customary Catholic ban on birth control. Another is the standard rural need for large families: children produce more than they consume, and therefore they provide an inexpensive source of needed farm labor. Today neither of these conditions holds, because the Catholic church has become more lenient with respect to birth control and because major farm equipment, and the need for a full education, make child labor unnecessary and impractical. Like other rural U.S. people, Cajuns today are reducing the size of their families. Nonetheless, Cajun families still remain large by contemporary U.S. standards—the birth rate in Louisiana has exceeded the national norm in every year since 1940—and children are still much desired (Statistical Abstract of Louisiana, 1981).

Babies receive constant attention and admiration, especially from women. If one member of a group of women has a baby with her, the conversation will invariably revolve around the child and around other children or grandchildren of the people present. Both mothers and fathers enjoy having their small children accompany them on errands and take great pride in the development and accomplishments of their small children. Because of the pivotal importance of children, it is rare for a social activity to exclude them. Parties invariably include children, who are expected to amuse themselves in appropriate fashion but who remain a constant topic of conversation.

In the past it was rare for Cajuns anywhere to complete high school; most went to work at a very young age on the family farm or business. Today most Cajuns do graduate from high school, with the result that in the past generation the high school years have taken on a great significance. Parents who lacked the opportunity to finish their educations place high hopes on their children, and because they can now afford to support their children through school they eagerly encourage school activities. The students, free from work responsibilities, participate in extracurricular if not the curricular activities with enthusiasm. While their grandparents (if not their parents) were working for a living as teenagers, teenagers in Henderson today are expected to enjoy their lives as much as they can with the full blessing of their parents.

The years before marriage are seen as the best years of a person's life. Courtship occurs at school or on dates and largely away from adult supervision. Like other teenagers in the United States, Henderson teenagers spend their dates at the movies, at nightclubs and dancehalls, or at school football games. Today it is not automatic that people will marry immediately after they graduate from high school; some go on to attend the university in Lafayette or elsewhere, while others get jobs and enjoy financial independence with no responsibilities. Especially for those with jobs and who live with their parents, this time is one of great freedom and pleasure.

Henderson residents are expected to marry young. In the past many were married as teenagers, and it is the rare middle-aged Henderson woman who did not have several children by the time she was 20. Today parents expect their children to finish school, and while many now marry right out of high school, many others prefer to wait. Nonetheless, a 21-year-old woman who is not married or engaged is considered to be getting old, and if she is not married by the time she is 25 her family has probably given up hope. Men are expected to be somewhat older at marriage, but not by much. One woman of 39 described the upcoming wedding of her 19-year-old daughter. When I suggested that 19 seems young to be getting married, she insisted that I was wrong:

> I was married at seventeen, and we're still together. The early marriages are the ones that last, because you grow up together. When you're in your mid-twenties or older that's too late, because you're already too independent by then.

There is some disagreement, though, about just how young a person should be at marriage. It is generally agreed that 25 is too old, but some adults now want their children to wait awhile after they complete high school. While the woman above was eager for her 19-year-old daughter to marry, another mother complained that her daughter was planning to marry as soon as she graduated from high school. This mother felt that her daughter should wait a few years and "have herself a good time before she settles down." Likewise, although young women are all in agreement that they should have their children as early as possible, older women sometimes wish they had waited. One middle-aged woman, when asked how old a first-time mother should be, said that it's not good to have children when you're too young because

> you should have your good time first. Get married, enjoy life, then have your kids. You should be anyway 22 before you have your kids.

Close family ties mean that throughout life people are never far from relatives. Cajuns have such strong ties to home and family that they are very reluctant to leave, and often go out of their way to arrange their lives in order to remain close to home. I myself was a constant source of pity because I had no family in the area. The emotional and physical closeness means that it is very rare for a Cajun not to have relatives to depend on, and it also means that it is virtually impossible to grow old alone. I have already discussed the Cajun dislike of nursing homes and other institutions. Very few elderly people in Henderson are not looked after by younger relatives.

Elderly people are highly respected throughout the area. Children are taught at an early age to respect their elders. They are admonished to refer to adults as "Miss Betty" or "Mr. Joe," and a child raised to refer to Joe Guidry as "Mr. Joe" will continue to call him "Mr. Joe" even when both are adults. Several community leaders are known as 'Mr. ——————" to everybody, out of respect for their age and experience. Even middle-aged, lifelong residents of the community will refer an inquiring anthropologist or other visitor to an elderly resident first, regardless of the nature of the question. Age implies wisdom and deserves respect, and it is assumed that the elderly know better.

Deceased relatives can be important in a household. Many households contain prominently displayed photographs of deceased parents, spouses, and sometimes children. When referring to a deceased parent, particularly in a critical way, people surround the reference with hedges, blessings, and compliments to make it clear they are not being disrespectful of the dead. "My poor old father, God rest him, was a hard worker and a wonderful man, but when he had a drink he used to . . ." is a characteristic way to refer to a deceased father's alcoholic excesses. The classified section of the St. Martin Parish weekly newspaper has a regular category for memorials, testimonials that families run on the anniversaries of the birth or death of a deceased relative. Frequently these memorials include photographs of the deceased and close with the words "sadly missed by" and a list of the survivors. Graves of relatives are kept scrupulously clean and neat and are visited regularly. A family that does not maintain their relatives' graves, particularly if they don't perform the annual whitewashing and cleanup for All Saints' Day (November 1), is said not to respect their dead. This is one of the most serious criticisms the community can level against one of its members.

SEX ROLES

It is expected in Henderson that men and women will have different interests and spheres of activity. Today many women hold jobs outside their homes, but it is understood that running the household is women's work and it is expected that women enjoy this kind of work more than men do. Even women who hold regular jobs and whose husbands work less regularly take full responsibility for domestic tasks. One woman, who holds a full-time job and whose husband works free-lance at whatever jobs he likes, still does all of the grocery shopping and cleaning at her house. When I asked why her husband doesn't help with these chores, she replied "because he works hard, and I don't mind." Another woman, also employed full time, was responsible for her house and children even during the months when her husband was unemployed and at home for much of the time. In contrast, outside work is considered a male activity, and most wives with jobs feel their own jobs are secondary to those of their husbands. Men are expected to perform outdoor chores around the house, and are expected to enjoy tinkering with machinery. Although there are some tasks and hobbies that are pursued by both men and women, in most respects the male and female worlds have little overlap.

From childhood, girls are raised to be interested in the home, to be "pretty," and to act "like a little lady." Boys are expected to prefer outdoor activities and are encouraged to fish and hunt with their fathers. Even as babies girls are frequently dressed in frills and ruffles, and their hair is sometimes set in curls according to the latest adult styles. One mother bought her three-year-old daughter a fur coat. In contrast, boys wear overalls and sneakers and are expected to get dirty when they play. It is understood that "boys will be boys," and to expect a boy to act like an adult is to rob him of his freedom.

Because small children spend much of their time at home with their mothers, and because women's hobbies and activities revolve around the home, boys require special training in masculine activities. Fathers take their sons hunting and fishing and buy small-gauge guns for their sons to use. By the time he is a teenager, a boy is expected to enjoy hunting and to want to go on independent hunting trips. Girls receive no similar formal training in female pastimes. A young girl may enjoy sewing her own clothes and may learn from her mother how to do this, but there is no community expectation that she do so. In general, the kinds of tasks expected of young women are solitary tasks such as cooking, sewing, and cleaning, and these are not things people can discuss or brag about. Preferred activities and hobbies for boys and men are much more clearly defined and conspicuous than they are for girls and women, and young children learn these differences early.

Traditionally, Cajun houses were arranged with the boys' bedroom (the *garconniere*) in the attic, reached by an outside staircase on the front porch. This provided young boys with the freedom to come and go with minimal parental knowledge or supervision. The girls slept in the main part of the house, sometimes in back of the parents' bedroom, where they were more closely supervised. This house plan is no longer in use, but the attitudes still apply. Teenage boys still have more freedom than girls, though girls today are beginning to demand more independence than they have had in the past. Boys have more access to the family car, especially at night. While they are not supposed to hang out at local bars, the penalties for a teenage boy doing this are far less severe than those for a girl. A girl who spends time in bars and getting drunk is considered "trash"; her brother might be viewed as "wild." Young men are expected to be a bit "wild" and to live somewhat dangerously; their female counterparts are expected to "have a good time," not a "wild" time. Mothers and fathers are more likely to enforce curfews for their teenage daughters than for their sons. Daughters may complain about their lack of freedom, but they do not expect to do whatever their brothers do and they know they will not be respected if they try.

Because most people live with their parents until marriage, marriage is a major change. Even for those who live adjacent to one set of parents, the establishment of a separate residence and the responsibilities that this implies can be a terrible shock. This change is profound for both men and women, but perhaps harder for women. Especially today, when many married women have jobs, marriage is not necessarily a financial burden on a man. Men's lives are less dramatically changed by marriage than are their wives': they move from the household run by their mother to that run by their wife. Married women are responsible for running the household. Although girls help their mothers with domestic tasks, they do not have firsthand responsibility until they themselves marry and take charge of their own home. It is the women, therefore, who have the more difficult transition. One young woman said that two weeks after she married she regretted it. "There's a lot you don't know about. There's some things you have to put up with that you didn't know about before, that nobody tells you." Men sometimes complain about the loss of independence, about having to report to their wives about their actions. But wives frequently do not enforce this, and even young husbands can often stay out as much as they want. Women find that they must suddenly be home whether or not they want to be; they must cook and clean as well as go to their regular jobs, and they are no longer able to spend as much time with their friends.

Men and women, especially if they are married, are not expected to be friends. Many Henderson residents have difficulty understanding the notion of male-female nonsexual friendships. Because in most cases men and women have different goals and concerns, they share few interests and there is little common ground for friendship. As a result, relations between men and women are generally assumed to be of a sexual nature whether or not they really are. In many cases people will avoid friendly contact with a person of the opposite sex out of fear of what people might think. In complaining about the tendency to gossip about male-female interactions, one man told me after we had conducted a lengthy interview that people were likely to talk about the amount of time he had spent with me. Because we had been in a public place (a restaurant) it is unlikely that such gossip would occur, but it is true that if a man and a woman married to other people spend much time together, people will probably talk about it. Although older people are generally exempt from this gossip, even they might take precautions to avoid it. One older widow sometimes receives assistance around her house from a retired married man who lives nearby. At one point she felt obligated to tell him not to visit her so often because "people might talk and it doesn't look right."

Because men and women are not expected to be friends, most interactions among adults are in single-sex groups. Groups of women get together to play cards, drink coffee, or just chat; groups of men hunt, fish, and hang out drinking coffee. In these groups, men discuss hunting and fishing trips, local politics, sex, and complain about their wives; women discuss their homes and families, clothes, sex, and complain about their husbands. There are few differences in the nature of the conversations, but neither sex would feel fully comfortable if a member of the opposite sex were present at these meetings. The exceptions to this pattern are among the elderly, who may congregate in mixed groups for various activities.

Generally speaking, men have greater freedom in their activities and personal lives than do their wives. Women must orient their lives around their families, which leaves them little time to themselves. Women rarely go on vacation without their husbands. One young woman expressed surprise when I visited my family alone, without my husband, over the Christmas holidays. She said her husband would never permit her to visit her family without him. I explained that in my case the trip cost several hundred dollars in air fare and that it was more practical for me to go alone. She replied that even under those circumstances her husband would not let her go alone:

> He's too jealous and possessive. He'd come with me anyway no matter how much it cost, or he wouldn't let me go. We wouldn't go unless we could both afford to go together. I just can't see him letting me ever go so far by myself.

Men, in contrast, go on long hunting trips with their friends, and many have jobs that take them away from home for long periods. In fact, men consider it their right to escape their families from time to time, and women do not interfere. Even on a day-to-day basis, women will interrupt their own activities to get home to prepare for the arrival of their children and husband, whereas men will continue with their activities until they are finished and will return home only when they are expected for a meal or when they want to be at home. When women get together to socialize it is most likely at someone's house. Occasionally a group of women will get together to go out to eat, but this is rare and is treated as a special occurrence. When men gather, it is usually in a public place such as a bar or one of the locally oriented restaurants. Men rarely meet at home just to pass the time.

Women are expected to be the guardians of family values, to instill mores and morals in their children. As such, they are expected to be more consistent in their church attendance and to enforce their children's attendance at church activities. Men go to church less regularly, but most consider themselves to be religious. They expect their children to attend church more regularly than they themselves do. Again, the exception to this is with older, retired men, who may participate in church activities as much as younger women do.

Women also take greater interest in school activities. It is they who see that homework gets done and who attend teacher conferences. Adult men and women are avid supporters of the local high school football team—sometimes more avid and energetic in their support than the students—but apart from athletics, men take little direct interest in school activities. They expect their children to attend and to do as well as possible, but they are not directly responsible for enforcing or supervising school activities.

It is only after retirement that men's and women's lives begin to converge. When men no longer have to go to work they spend more time around the house, sometimes helping their wives with domestic chores. Because their husbands no longer work, wives are relieved of the obligation to take care of their husbands "because he works so hard." Retired men involve themselves more in church activities and spend more time drinking coffee with their friends during the day. Because their activities begin to overlap, and because of their age, older men and women can visit one another without necessarily provoking comment. After retirement is also when husbands and wives can spend time together and develop common interests. Couples who can afford it may travel for the first time or may undertake other joint ventures. The release of men from the responsibilities of work breaks down the barriers between men and women, often for the only period in their lives.

THE PERPETUATION OF CAJUN CULTURE

The household is where children learn the basic values of their family, community, and culture. In Henderson, a town caught between the traditional Cajun culture and the outside U.S. one, this has important implications. At home or with relatives and close friends is where a Cajun child learns the differences between Cajuns and other U.S. citizens. Children learn that their culture is a private one that is little valued in the world beyond Acadiana except as a curiosity. They learn when and how it is appropriate to act Cajun, and they pass this information on to their own children. The family is, then, the guardian of the culture. This is especially true today when outside pressures are making traditional Cajun culture less and less viable.

What little French a child hears today is likely to be spoken at home or among kin. English has become the language used in public and formal contexts; French persists in some domestic contexts and in small business transactions made among close associates. French has become the language of intimacy and emotion, used at home by adults when they argue or when they don't want their children to understand what they say, or by relatives in close personal interaction. This is especially true among young parents today because they were raised predominantly in English and are not fully comfortable speaking French. A child in Henderson learns that French is not appropriate for use on the outside and by extension that Cajun culture is appropriate in domestic and certain very restricted public contexts but not in dealing with the outside world or with strangers.

Traditionally, the Cajun mother was the principal transmitter of the culture because she had primary responsibility for raising her children. A mother's role was more powerful in the past than it is today because formal education used to be rare. Lacking teachers to serve as role models and to teach them values that might conflict with those of their parents, children learned virtually everything from their mothers. This pattern was compounded by the many non-Cajun men who settled in the area over the years and married Cajun women. Because most of these men did not speak French and were unfamiliar with the local culture, their children learned the language and the culture from their mothers. This was never the norm—most Cajun women have always married Cajun men—but to the extent that intermarriage occurred, it reinforced the already strong tendency for the culture to be transmitted through women.

Today that pattern has changed. Children are still raised principally by their mothers, but women's values have changed and many no longer consider traditional Cajun culture to be advantageous. Women today are concerned with outside prestige and success, and they know that the success of their children depends on full proficiency in English. They also know that in the larger towns of the area a heavy French accent is a sign of "backwardness" and that Henderson residents have long been mocked for their accents and their strong reliance on the local dialect of French. Women are also aware that for generations their families had little access to the consumer goods of the outside society. Now that they have the money to spend, they are eager to own the goods that will mark them as prosperous and contemporary rather than poor and backward. As a result, women today are transmitting to their children the values and habits of the larger U.S. society.

In contrast, Cajun men are less concerned with outside prestige and more concerned with their prestige within the community. Men also enjoy possessing consumer goods, but their emphasis is on things they can use among themselves: guns, boats, fishing equipment, and other hobby gear. Especially for men in Henderson, most of whom work outdoors in the local area rather than in offices in nearby cities, the prestige structure of the larger towns is of little concern. Like their wives, they know they are sometimes mocked for their accents and their language; but as long as they don't have to deal directly with the people who scorn them, they don't take action to alter their habits. Indeed, some young men today are taking an arrogant pride in their heritage and in the fact that they share a tradition different from that of the U.S. majority. They relish the reputation Cajuns have acquired as a rough and wild people. To this group, proficiency in French is a sign of prestige, a kind of reverse snobbery that glorifies a stigma. Other observers of the area have noted that while young women who speak French are seen as unsophisticated and undesirable, their male counterparts may deliberately attempt to learn more French as a kind of male code language when they take a first job (Tentchoff 1977). The net effect is that among the younger generations, traditional Cajun culture is more apparent among men than among women, and it is men who are more likely to transmit this culture to their children.

Other aspects of the culture are preserved at home besides the language. While the use of French appears to be on the decline, traditional cooking is not. At home is where children eat most of their meals and where they learn about Cajun food. Such things as gumbo, boiled crawfish, and squirrel jambalaya are staples in the Henderson diet. Food is important to Cajun culture. Visitors are always offered at least a cup of coffee and often a meal, and no family reunion is complete without a large meal that can last most of the day. Cajuns are proud of their food, and this is a sentiment that children learn very early in life.

Food and cooking are largely the domain of women, who cook traditional Cajun foods regularly. In larger cities like Lafayette, traditional Cajun cuisine has become a self-conscious statement about ethnic identity; this attitude also prevails at most of the tourist-oriented restaurants in Henderson. In Henderson homes, by contrast, Cajun food is simply the kind of food people eat, and it is cooked and eaten out of choice and authentic tradition and not as a self-conscious statement. In this regard women play a larger role in the perpetuation of the culture than they do with respect to the language. But Henderson women are beginning to experiment with other forms of cooking, especially because they can buy ready-made convenience foods in their supermarkets. Today many Cajun women cook other kinds of foods at least as often as they do Cajun food. Cajun men enjoy cooking and are often quite proud of their culinary accomplishments. Men rarely do the regular family cooking, but they like to cook the game they hunt and virtually anything in large quantities for parties. When men cook, they are most likely to cook traditional foods like gumbos or to boil the crawfish for a crawfish boil. Men rarely experiment with exotic or prepackaged convenience foods. Here too, then, the culture is more dependably (though more sporadically) being transmitted by men.

This suggests that the future of authentic Cajun traditions lies with men rather than with women. This does not mean that the culture is dying or that it is becoming exclusively male. As old traditions die new ones develop, and it is arbitrary and unfair to declare that women no longer are participants in Cajun culture. What appears to be happening is that women are adhering less to old traditions and are developing some new ones. Men are more faithful to the old, and the result is a new variety of culture that is neither the old Cajun culture nor the current U.S. one. This new culture will also be transmitted by the family, where members will make decisions concerning the utility of certain culture traits in their lives. Cajuns remain strongly family oriented—this is one trait that persists among women at least as much as among men—and the strength of the family will not diminish any time soon.

6/Social life

In a community like Henderson, social interactions require adjustments, compromises, and a recognition of individual personality quirks. Because Henderson is such a small town, social interactions occur among the same people over and over, and invariably people must deal with others with whom they don't get along or would prefer to avoid. As a result, the residents have developed ways to accommodate one another and to ensure reasonably peaceful coexistence in most situations.

BASIC SOCIAL INTERACTIONS

Cajuns have long been known for their warmth, hospitality, and gregariousness. Henderson residents posseses all of these traits, and their generosity can sometimes be overwhelming to an urban outsider not accustomed to it. It is almost impossible to visit a household without eating, or at the very least without drinking coffee. Coffee is offered to all visitors, and many households keep fresh coffee ready all day for visitors who might stop by. It can be hazardous to visit too many households in one day because of the amount of coffee one may be expected to drink. (Cajun coffee is thick and strong and sometimes sweetened in the pot. I have never found Cajun coffee too strong for my taste, but many outsiders have trouble with it.) To refuse an offer of something to eat or drink is not considered rude, as it is in some cultures, but most Cajuns feel they are better hosts if their guest is drinking or eating something. As a result, food and drink are pressed on a visitor, who will probably find it difficult to refuse.

The insistence on serving a guest extends well beyond the offering of food and drink. In the Henderson area, a "stranger" who is liked may be given food to take home. The first time I visited Robert and Louise Theriot, they gave me a large package of crawfish tails from their freezer. They insisted that I take it, gave me advice on how to cook it, and checked with me afterward to make certain that my husband and I had enjoyed it. Buck Wyatt and his wife took me crawfishing in their pond early one morning after serving me coffee at their house. I contributed nothing to the day save my extra weight in their boat and the questions I kept asking as they worked. When we returned to their house (and drank more coffee), Mr. Wyatt gave me a package of wild ducks from the freezer, which he and his sons had hunted. He apologized for giving me ducks instead of crawfish, but he said the crawfish weren't good enough to give away (it was early in the season).

This treatment, of course, is not extended to all casual visitors. Coffee is served routinely to anybody who is welcomed into the house, but bounty from the freezer is not. This is reserved for family or selected "strangers": those who are liked and who are considered important. Because I was writing a book I was "important" by definition. Because I took the time to listen to what my hosts had to say—indeed my whole purpose was to listen to them—I was generally liked. The gifts were my hosts' way of thanking me for letting them speak.

Henderson residents are thankful for the opportunity to have their say because they have been ignored and castigated for so long. Because Henderson was known for so long as the "end of the road" and its citizens as ignorant swampers, many residents expect outsiders, especially visitors, to perpetuate the stereotype. One native refers to this as the "great shame": Cajuns in general, and Henderson residents in particular, were insulted and put down for so long that they have almost come to believe the insults themselves, and they make special concessions to outsiders in order to create a favorable impression. As a result, it is not uncommon for a "stranger" to be tested for reliability and trustworthiness before being taken into full confidence. Many residents retain a certain degree of suspicion of all outsiders, assuming guilt until convinced otherwise.

Some younger residents have become cynical about the many journalists, writers, and tourists who pass through asking questions. They have become almost hostile to outsiders, whom they see no need to accommodate. When I first met Paul Benoit, he told me that people in Henderson waterski on the backs of alligators and that children use their alligators as transportation to and from school. He had assumed that I, like many writers, was new in the area and staying for only a few days, and he wanted to play a trick on one of the people whom he felt would only insult or misunderstand his town. (He was surprised when I asked him, in French, to demonstrate the skiing and to show me his pet alligators.) The net effect, however, is the same: outsiders are to be trusted only after they have proven themselves worthy.

Common techniques used to verify the trustworthiness of an outsider range from speaking in French to asking direct questions about personal background. Because Henderson residents know the details of one another's lives so well, it is considered appropriate to ask questions of an outsider whose life is unknown. Questions concerning marital status are asked especially of women, as are questions concerning husband's occupation and children. Place of residence is also important, because this can indicate certain attitudes the visitor might hold. It was frequently assumed that I lived in Lafayette or even farther away, which would suggest I could not possibly understand or sympathize with the intricacies of life in a small, rural, Cajun town. People were consistently surprised when I told them I lived in Breaux Bridge, especially when they learned that I had been raised as a "Yankee." That I had lived in Breaux Bridge for several years increased my credibility.

In Henderson, then, visitors are greeted with warmth and generosity if they are respected and trusted and with suspicion bordering on hostility if they are not. Similar attitudes prevail with respect to one another. The ubiquitous pot of coffee is kept warm in all households for welcome drop-in guests. "Let's drink coffee" and "Come have coffee" are standard invitations issued to friends. However, personal grudges and feuds do occur among residents. In fact, Henderson residents can hold grudges for extraordinarily long periods of time. Leila Stelly and Mrs. Lionel Theriot have ignored one another as a result of an incident that occurred almost 40 years ago; to this day they will not speak and refuse to acknowledge one another's presence when they find themselves together at a social event. Likewise, Denise LeBlanc, now in her thirties, was angry when an old high school rival asked her for a favor. Jenny Hebert is employed at Peltier's grocery, where she frequently prepares the meat. One customer refuses to accept meat when Jenny is working because they had a disagreement several years ago and have not spoken to one another since. In order to avoid dealing with Jenny, the customer asks other store employees to package her meat for her. Fernand Broussard is a strong opponent of Pat .Huval, the town's mayor. He has actively worked on behalf of candidates running against Pat and the candidates Pat supports. While Broussard declines to explain why he opposes Pat, his daughter suggested that it is because Pat claims credit for having first served crawfish in his restaurant, and Broussard maintains that he served crawfish at his club before Pat did. If this is the reason for the feud, this rivalry is now 30 years old.

The easiest way for rivals to deal with their mutual dislike is to avoid contact with one another. This can be difficult in such a small town, but it is not impossible, as demonstrated by the examples of Mrs. Stelly and Mrs. Theriot and of Jenny Hebert and the meat customer. However, these conflicts can interfere with the smooth progression of social life by affecting others in the community besides those officially involved. For example, for several years two families were engaged in a feud that began with a paternity suit. This was a private matter between two families, affecting their relations with one another but not with anybody else. However, one member happened to be a policeman who responded to a minor accident at the home of the opposing family and was shot during the course of the investigation. As a result, the feud got out of hand and eventually involved the entire town. For several months relations in town were colored by people's involvement with the two families in question, and it became difficult for any social interactions to occur outside the context of this particular problem.

In general, then, Henderson residents are simultaneously warm and suspicious. They can make a visitor feel like family, or they can quarrel, refuse to cooperate, and hold grudges for long periods of time. All of these traits are products of small town life: the necessity to deal with all kinds of people in many contexts requires tolerance and warmth in most situations, but it can also reduce patience and make for short tempers when such adjustments become impossible.

Because Henderson was founded by swamp fishers, it traditionally lacked the local elite that was part of so many other Cajun communities. The bourgeois merchants in the area were concentrated in Breaux Bridge, where Henderson residents traditionally transacted much of their business. Even the local fish market owners and other small merchants in Henderson shared the swamper peasant background with their customers, and so did not comprise a local elite. As everywhere, some families were always better off than others (one native in his forties describes his childhood preference for visiting the house of a particular neighborhood friend because there was always Coca Cola to drink). Nonetheless, the differences in prosperity were minor, and most people considered themselves to be poor and hardworking.

This is no longer the case. Just about everybody can now afford Coca Cola. Some households have acquired a degree of prosperity previously unknown in the community. A drive through Henderson reveals marked differences in the size and luxury of houses, cars, and other possessions. Today the most desirable houses are the ones with swimming pools, video cassette recorders, and Cadillacs, not those with store-bought ice cream and soft drinks.

Despite the new differences in wealth, residents expect those who have more to act as humbly as those who have less. It is acceptable to spend money conspicuously, but not to act better than anybody else because of having money. Social equality among economic unequals is expected, and wealthy residents who act "stuck up" are scorned. In Henderson a wealthy person is likely to be the sibling of one who is considerably less well off due to differences in business successes, personal ambition, or luck. The greatest praise one can give wealthy people is to say they are "just like anybody else"; conversely, to say a rich person thinks he or she is better than anybody else is harsh criticism.

As a result, Henderson remains a remarkably egalitarian community. Those with less may envy those with more, but they may also be good friends. Today there is a small merchant elite, but this group lacks the power the nineteenth-century Cajun merchants in other communities had because by now virtually all residents are educated and can take care of their own interactions with the outside. The new economic elite is an elite only in terms of income and possessions, not in terms of prestige, popularity, or power.

ORGANIZATIONS AND ASSOCIATIONS

Social anthropologists have long maintained that a community is held together in large part by its constituent clubs, organizations, and other institutions that can claim competing loyalties. Following Max Gluckman (1955), it is accepted that these groups form sets of cross-cutting ties and obligations that make it difficult for an individual to break free of the responsibilities and privileges of group membership. This is deemed true especially in complex societies in which kinship obligations do not regulate all aspects of social life and in which individuals require artificial bonds to hold themselves together in a cohesive group.

Like any community, Henderson has its share of these organizations. They vary widely in formality and structure, in prominence, and in membership and participation. Some are regarded as being of critical importance to the community, while others are less highly thought of. Collectively, these groups represent the interests of the town's residents and indicate the amount and the context of nonkin-based cooperative action.

Organizations, or voluntary associations as they are widely called in the anthropological literature, are less prominent in Henderson than in many other U.S. communities. There are several reasons for this. As noted, voluntary associations are most common where kinship ties cannot take care of all of the needs of the populace. Although in Henderson it is not prescribed that family members act cooperatively, it is generally expected that they will and these expectations are almost always met. There is accordingly a lesser need to depend on the assistance of collectivities of friends or casual acquaintances. And because "everybody is related" in Henderson, kinship provides its own set of ties that keep the community functioning; organizations to maintain community spirit or morale are not necessary.

Compounding the extensive kin ties in Henderson is a spirit of independence. Cajuns in general are an independent, self-reliant people who dislike relying on outsiders for help or advice. This independence appears to be stronger in Henderson than in some of its neighboring communities, perhaps because of the extensive kin ties that make it possible to eschew outside interference, or perhaps as a vestige of life in the swamps, which required a kind of solitary independence. Whatever the cause, Henderson residents firmly believe that people should not be obligated to cooperate or to structure their activities according to the wishes of an organization. Although residents freely help one another with specific chores, this willingness to help out is a product of the voluntary nature of the aid. Organizations that require communal labor are resented as invading personal privacy and as infringing on individual rights.

As a result, Henderson contains no general-purpose service organizations designed for community improvements. Neighboring Breaux Bridge boasts chapters of several such groups, including the American Legion, the Lions, and several veterans' groups. Breaux Bridge is a bigger town with less extensive kin ties than Henderson, and it may be that these groups are more necessary there; also, Breaux Bridge residents are generally more willing to make personal sacrifices for group benefit. For example, Breaux Bridge residents are more willing than are those in Henderson to abide by zoning and other regulations that may restrict individual freedom for the good of the community. In Henderson social service organizations cannot become established. Over the years several enterprising young businessmen have attempted to form Henderson chapters of the Jaycees (Junior Chamber of Commerce), and all of these efforts have failed. In 1983 a small Jaycee group was formed, but because the leader could never get anybody to attend the meetings, he was forced to abandon the project.

Special-purpose interest groups do crop up from time to time in Henderson to address specific needs. Groups of business owners may join together to address an issue of concern to them. For example, in 1983 a group of crawfish processors, together with a scientist from one of the state universities, formed a company to extract and market a red dye from crawfish shells. For several months interested people met regularly to arrange the details of the project. Once the business was established, however, the meetings stopped and joint enterprises among the crawfish processors came to a halt. The strike of crawfishers was successful temporarily, but support was far from unanimous and almost immediately there were some fishers who violated the terms of the strike. The fishers simply could not be persuaded to work together rather than independently. In Henderson, cooperative interest groups generally last only until a specific task is completed, at which time the groups dissolve.

The groups that do maintain continuity over time are those that provide a major public service. The volunteer fire department, for example, has no difficulty attracting members. It is composed of men of varying ages who join for equally varying reasons: some to gain a network of allies for use in a political career; some for the strictly humanitarian reasons of fire protection; others for the companionship and for something to do. Meetings are typically casual and loosely structured. Often they are delayed while someone goes to buy beer for the group, and they are always followed by a supper cooked at the fire station by one of the members (the firemen in Henderson are excellent cooks). The atmosphere at these meetings suggests that even the fire department might have trouble obtaining cooperation from its members if it were not for the very important issue of fire protection—and for the beer and the food.

The fire department and the paid police department each has a small ladies' auxiliary composed principally of the wives of the men in the department. The main functions of these groups are fundraising, and they do not hold regular meetings. In addition there is a group called Friends of the Police, which is composed of friends, relatives, and supporters of the police department and the chief, who is engaged in a chronic and bitter series of disputes with the town's mayor. This group raises funds and provides moral support in what is essentially a political battle between two community leaders. Although more visible than the ladies' auxiliaries and other groups in Henderson, the Friends of the Police also lacks regular meetings and a stable membership, and it is mobilized only in a crisis when the police department needs allies.

There are other small clubs and loosely structured social groups, but these tend to be groups of friends and/or relatives who meet for purely recreational ends. Men belong to hunting clubs; women may have a regular group of friends with whom they play cards. These cannot truly be considered interest groups and they do little to promote the unity of the town because membership is flexible and because, by definition, they are comprised of people who would cooperate with one another anyway. Generally speaking, social life in Henderson is regulated by kinship, individual personality, and by the mere fact of being from Henderson rather than a neighboring community.

RELIGION AND CHURCH GROUPS

Although residents are strongly independent, religion plays a very important part in the life of Henderson. Church groups might be the strongest interest groups in town. Even those residents who do not participate actively in church organizations consider themselves to be deeply religious. More than any other institution, the church (or churches, as there are two of them) can claim the full loyalty of everybody and can truly command group action and support.

Cajuns have traditionally been Catholic; in fact one of the reasons for the original expulsion from Acadia in Canada was that they refused to abandon Catholicism for the Anglican church. The Catholic church has strongly colored many aspects of Cajun culture, a point discussed at greater length in Chapter 9. In the past many Cajun communities were only minimally served by priests, and often the people were forced to depend on themselves and on folk ideas for spiritual guidance. This was especially true in the most remote areas, such as the swamps where Henderson residents originally lived. Today anybody who wants to attend church has ready access, and Catholicism as practiced in Louisiana differs little from that practiced elsewhere in the world. In most communities the church is the most conspicuous building in town (sometimes rivalled by a city hall or courthouse), and it is the one that commands the most respect.

Some larger communities have two Catholic churches. This is a vestige of segregation, when whites and blacks had separate facilities for everything. Separate churches remain in towns with populations large enough to sustain both, but in most cases there is some mixing of the congregations. In Breaux Bridge the two churches have different mass schedules, allowing people to choose whichever is more convenient. During Lent, a busy white woman in Breaux Bridge attended services every morning at the black church because it fit her schedule better; likewise, blacks will attend the white church when it suits them. One white Breaux Bridge woman goes to the black church intermittently simply for the variety. It is rare, though, for a person to attend the "other race" church on a regular basis; most will attend occasionally according to their convenience but maintain regular membership in the church of their own race.

Henderson contains a single Catholic church, which serves the town and a surrounding rural area. The parishioners are predominantly white, though blacks and Vietnamese do attend. Because there are so few blacks in the Henderson area, they cannot support their own church. Most attend the black churches in nearby Breaux Bridge or Cecilia. The Vietnamese, who have no church of their own, use the one in Henderson, which is most convenient to them.

All children in the Henderson area are baptized and sent to religion classes, and most are confirmed. Even parents who do not attend church have their children baptized. As a result, religion is an integral part of the upbringing of area children, and it remains with most adults throughout their lives. The doctrines taught in religion class are internalized and become part of the general morality of the people. Betty LeBlanc, who is in her twenties and was raised in Henderson, told me of a dilemma she faced before she was married almost ten years ago. She did not want to have sexual intercourse with her fiance before they married because she knew it would be a sin to do so. He told her he would have to either "get it somewhere else, or do it himself," both of which she knew would also be sins in the eyes of the church. She finally told him

to take care of his own problem. Whatever he did, if he did anything, it would be a sin in any case. I figured if he wanted to badly enough he would do it anyway no matter what I did. I decided that if he wanted to sin that was his business, but he wasn't going to make me sin with him.

This is not to suggest that young Henderson women do not engage in premarital sex. They do, as evidenced by their illegitimate children. But this woman's dilemma illustrates the effect of church teachings on everyday life.

Church services are obligatory for weddings and funerals, as well as for baptism and confirmation. Cajuns generally believe that a marriage is not legitimate if it has not been sanctified by the church. In a community near Henderson, a young couple chose not to have a church wedding and were married by a local judge. An old family friend wanted to give them a reception, but she was afraid that the marriage was not legitimate and did not want to contribute to a sinful union. After receiving permission from her priest and the assurance that the marriage was not a sinful one, she held the reception at her home. Even today, when divorce has become more common, some divorced persons believe that their marriages are permanent in the eyes of God.

Not all adults attend church regularly. However, many of those who do not still insist that they are religious. In Henderson it is assumed that most people are Catholic no matter how regularly they attend church. This may be a vestige of the times when church services were not available; the old community of Atchafalaya, and the rural area surrounding where Henderson is now, received church services only once a month prior to the 1940s. Weekly church attendance is therefore not a requisite component of religious feeling.

This is especially true for men, who are not expected to attend church as regularly as women. However, it also holds for women, not all of whom are satisfied with current church conditions but who are nonetheless highly religious according to their own standards. One middle-aged woman admits that she does not attend church regularly, but insists that she believes in God and is a religious person. This same woman gave a large gold cross pendant as a gift to a close friend who also does not attend church regularly. Even the local Catholic priest acknowledges that many who attend church may not be truly devout, and that those who do not attend may be more religious in their own ways than some regular attendees.

Catholicism is so important, even in secular life, that the presence of the church is felt at all times. Virtually all homes in the Henderson area have small religious icons scattered throughout: prayers affixed to bathroom mirrors and kitchen walls, crucifixes hanging over doorways, reproductions of Leonardo da Vinci's famous Last Supper fresco. Many homes have statues of the Virgin Mary in the front yard. The woman who gave her friend the gold cross pendant, and the friend who received it, both have these religious emblems in their homes despite their irregular church attendance. These emblems of Catholicism are so prevalent that, although they are frequently taken for granted, they provide people with a sense of order. They become part of the general background, not noticed until they are missing. When I first moved to Breaux Bridge, I rented a small house that contained many of these Catholic images. Not being Catholic myself, I removed them from the walls and put them away, to replace when I moved out. One evening I was visited by a Henderson native who had lived in several other parts of the United States and who was familiar with my personal religious convictions. After a while he said, unsolicited and out of context,

Religious statue on front lawn. This house is located on the Henderson main road.

I know what's wrong with your house. It's been bothering me that there's something that doesn't seem right about it. I just figured it out. You don't have any crosses over the doorways. It doesn't look right without crosses over the doorways.

In many ways, the local priest is the most respected person in town. Priests are always referred to as "Father," even on social occasions with long-term friends, and are treated formally and deferentially regardless of their age or length of tenure. When the Henderson priest attended a political rally in 1983, the audience stood as he entered the room; not even the political candidates being honored received such respect. Cajuns are remarkably tolerant of the personality quirks of their priests, and are willing to admit openly which priests they like and which they dislike. They discuss with great candor their opinions of the priests' personalities, personal styles, and whether a given priest may at one time have had a girlfriend. But despite their frankness about their priests' personalities, even a priest who is unpopular is treated with the utmost respect by virtue of his title.

The church in Henderson fulfills important social functions in addition to its religious, moral, and spiritual ones. There are several community organizations affiliated with the church, some of which are every bit as social as they are religious. The Catholic church has two choirs, a Ladies' Altar Society, and a Holy Name Society for men. Each of these groups holds social functions in addition to the work they perform for the church. Membership is relatively constant, although there has been some factionalism in the choir, resulting in the formation of a second choir. Members of these groups remain active for many years, seeing the organizations not just as ways to serve the church but also as ways to keep busy and enjoy themselves. Mrs. Trahan, a member of one of the choirs, explained that she enjoys it because

> I like the music, and I like the people. It's a lot of my friends in there. We sometimes go eat out at one of the restaurants after choir practice, and it's a chance to get together.

These groups are mostly composed of older people, who are more likely to have the leisure time to devote to church activities. Both choirs are made up almost exclusively of senior women, and the members of the Holy Name Society are all senior men. Younger men have little to do with organized church activities. The Ladies' Altar Society is more mixed in age, containing several younger women with children as well as some older ones.

The Catholic church is only one of two churches in Henderson, though it is by far the predominant one. In 1975 a group of Henderson area residents broke from the Catholic church and formed a Bible church, which has been increasing in membership over the years. This church teaches a strict interpretation of the Bible, claiming that the Bible contains all the information God intended people to know. Most of the members are white, though there are a few black families who attend from time to time. Many are not Cajun and were not originally Catholic; rather, they are people from other states who have recently moved to the area and who were members of similar churches in their previous homes.

This church maintains an extremely active membership and conducts regular prayer meetings and Bible study sessions. Only about half of the members live in the Henderson area. The others come from communities as far as 30 miles away. Because so many of its members live so far from Henderson, the impact of the Bible church on the local community is limited. Nonetheless, the Bible church is conspicuous because of the fervor of its members. Although they do not actively proselytize, Bible church members are extremely devout. Like the local Catholics, they have religious icons decorating their houses, but they tend to have more of them and to keep them more prominently displayed. One of the founders of this church owns a fish-processing plant, the outside wall of which is decorated with a mural depicting Jesus and the disciples fishing. Whereas local Catholics may have so internalized their religion that they are not consciously aware of the extent of its effects on their day-to-day decisions, Bible church members actively model their behavior according to the dictates of their religion. As a result, they are noticeable and are sometimes considered to be religious fanatics by others in the community.

Bible church members from the Henderson area still have Catholic relatives, and in some families there is tension concerning the subject of religion. Family relations sometimes suffer as a result of conversion. Catholic relatives may feel betrayed, insulted, or may consider their converted kin to be strange. Bible church members claim that their friends and relatives do not understand them and that some were offended when they chose to change their religion. One woman complained that her relatives didn't understand when she and her husband stopped drinking

Mural on the place of business owned by the founder of the Henderson Bible church. The mural depicts Jesus and two disciples fishing.

alcohol. Nonetheless, Bible church members are recognized within the community for what they are and are respected or disrespected as anyone else might be. Church membership is treated as just another personality variable, a quirk that must be understood and dealt with in order for business as usual to continue. The Bible church member who owns the fishing plant is highly respected for his honesty, his good disposition, and for how hard he works. Another Bible church member was described to me as having been

> no good before, and he's no good now. He just thinks he's better because he changed to that church. But he's always been a bum, and he's still a bum, no matter what he says about that Jesus stuff.

There is little active conflict between the two churches: the Catholics consider the Bible group to be slightly eccentric but harmless fanatics, and the Bible group consider the Catholics to be unsaved, misguided, and therefore pitiable. Henderson Catholics maintain that Cajuns raised as Catholics would join the Bible church only if they were somewhat strange to begin with or if they had been rejected by the Catholic church and needed an alternative. Indeed, one member was divorced and therefore unable to receive communion in the Catholic church. Afraid that she might go to Hell, she was converted to a new religion that allows her the opportunity for salvation. Another had been raised Baptist, married a Catholic, and was disappointed when a local Catholic priest refused to baptize her children. At that point she converted to the Bible church, which permitted her and her family full privileges.

Both churches are singularly able to elicit cooperation from these otherwise fiercely independent people. Although Henderson residents strongly oppose any form of taxation, they give willingly and generously to their churches. Neither church has trouble raising funds or assistance for projects of any kind. As I will discuss in the next chapter, governmental authority of any kind is rejected as unreasonable, as is any attempt to organize behavior. The authority most respected and accepted in Henderson is the authority of the church (whichever church that may be), and this authority is accepted without question or doubt. As a result, religion is the most powerful institution in the community and the one most able to elicit cooperative action among community members.

WHITES, BLACKS, AND VIETNAMESE

The above descriptions of social life apply predominantly to the white Cajun majority population of the Henderson area. While there has always been some inequality between the white majority and the black minority in Henderson, in general relations within the community are good. White residents often deny that blacks live there. This initially confused me, because I saw several black households in the area. When I asked questions such as, "If there are no black people in Henderson, tell me about the —————— family [a local black family]," the most common answer was "Well, those are some good colored people. All our colored people here are good, we get along well and have no trouble." In other words, white Henderson residents assume that blacks make bad neighbors, and because their "colored" neighbors are good they are not black like the others.

In fact, although there are severe economic and social discrepancies between the two races, there are many friendships as well. Two Henderson widows, one white and one black, consider themselves to be best friends. Whites and blacks have worked side by side for years and get along extremely well. A black deputy sheriff hangs out with the white owners of one of the restaurants and is welcomed as a friend when he arrives. Whites sometimes feel that they have to explain or justify these relationships, but the friendships are real.

In addition to the white majority and the black minority, who share most aspects of culture and who form a more or less unified group, there is another population in Henderson that maintains its own set of social relations. This group, the Vietnamese, is not fully integrated into Henderson social life despite the fact that they live and work in town. Neither whites nor blacks socialize much with the Vietnamese, and while whites defend the reputations of their black neighbors, they are less solicitous of the Vietnamese.

The first Vietnamese refugees arrived in 1975. Before moving to Henderson, most had been in another community in Louisiana where they had been sponsored by the local Catholic priest. When the priest was transferred to Breaux Bridge, the Vietnamese moved with him. Many settled in Henderson rather than in Breaux Bridge because they were able to get jobs in the seafood plants and wanted to live within walking distance of their jobs. The Vietnamese community in Henderson (and in some surrounding communities, including Breaux Bridge) has grown so that today Henderson contains roughly 100 Vietnamese, or about 6 percent of the population of the town. This is a small number, but the Vietnamese are highly conspicuous by virtue of physical appearance and language.

During the early days of their settlement in the Henderson area, the Vietnamese were deeply resented by the Cajun natives of the community. Vietnamese refugees received financial benefits from the U.S. government and were given jobs and assistance in resettlement. Cajuns, independent and resentful of any kind of governmental interference, objected that they had never had federal assistance when they were poor and that their ancestors had carved out their prosperity without benefit of food stamps and welfare (the Cajuns overlooked the free land grants their ancestors had received when they arrived in Louisiana). In addition, those area residents who had fought in Vietnam were accustomed to seeing Vietnamese as the enemy and found it difficult to accept former enemies as neighbors. As a result, relations between the two groups have never been fully amicable.

The Vietnamese community is a heterogeneous one, composed of North as well as South Vietnamese, former urban professionals and rural peasants, French speakers and those who speak only Vietnamese. Initially, the Vietnamese attempted to retain some of their own former class structure, but because they were classified as Vietnamese with no regard for internal distinctions, these distinctions became impossible to maintain. There now appears to be little internal stratification within the Vietnamese community despite the differences that were present before they settled in this country.

Today Vietnamese are resented in Henderson for reasons beyond those of the early years. Large numbers of Vietnamese are employed in the fish-processing plants, where jobs are always available even for unskilled labor and where the language barrier is not a problem. Vietnamese workers consistently outperform their Cajun counterparts, and as a result they are preferred by some of the plant owners and are able to make more money. Some Cajun workers accuse the Vietnamese of being greedy because they will work on weekends, will work multiple shifts in one day, and work quickly. They are sometimes accused of having no pride, largely because Vietnamese men work in seafood plants at jobs Cajuns consider suitable only for women. For their part, Vietnamese workers say that they see in the seafood industry an opportunity to improve their lives in this country, to gain the advantages of other U.S. residents who have started with something more than what they had. This lack of understanding has resulted in resentment on both sides, as each group perceives the other as selfish and lacking respect.

Despite the physical and linguistic differences that make the Vietnamese so conspicuous, they are not as different from their Cajun neighbors as many might believe. Like the Cajuns, most of the Vietnamese are Catholic and were so before they arrived in the United States. (One Vietnamese high school student estimated that there might be two Vietnamese families in Henderson who are not Catholic.) Their homes are decorated with the same Catholic religious icons as are those of their Cajun neighbors. They work as fishers, peelers, kitchen help in restaurants, and as skilled and semiskilled laborers—occupations shared by their Cajun neighbors. Some Vietnamese were educated in French. In addition, both Henderson Cajuns and Vietnamese are now experiencing a wave of prosperity for the first time, and both groups share certain values with respect to the accumulation of money and consumer goods. (There are important differences here as well. Vietnamese do not understand the U.S. economic practice of going into debt and cannot comprehend why so many of their neighbors buy things they cannot pay for. Vietnamese, rather than taking out loans, will accumulate large stores of cash that they use to purchase the consumer goods they want. As a result, the Cajuns see the Vietnamese as hoarders, while the Vietnamese see the Cajuns as spendthrifts. Nonetheless, the desire to spend money on consumer goods remains constant.) There are differences among the two groups as well, but these differences are not nearly as great as many might think.

Personal socializing between the two populations is minimal. There are few interethnic friendships in school despite the fact that all Henderson residents attend the same schools. Some of the Vietnamese fish peelers who are proficient in English are friendly with their Cajun coworkers, but these friendships are generally restricted to the workplace. With few exceptions, Cajuns and Vietnamese do not visit one another at home or socialize together away from work.

Although Cajuns stress the importance of social equality among economic unequals, this principle does not cross racial lines. No Vietnamese in Henderson is truly wealthy (nor is any black), but many are the economic equals of many of their Cajun neighbors. But regardless of economic status, Henderson Cajuns do not view the Vietnamese as their social equals and do not want to fraternize with them. In Henderson the Vietnamese are treated as a people apart, for whom the regular rules of social interaction do not apply.

Despite generally cool relations between the two groups, over the years there have been a few Cajun-Vietnamese marriages. The Vietnamese welcome this, explaining that "it's the American way." Because both groups are Catholic, the conflicts are not as great as they might appear. Vietnamese are concerned, however, about the high U.S. divorce rate, which they perceive as a violation of Catholicism and of their cultural traditions. Nonetheless, the Vietnamese welcome these mixed couples. Cajuns are more sympathetic to marriages involving Cajun men and Vietnamese women than to the reverse, but generally they frown on these marriages. In one such case, a Cajun woman who had married a Vietnamese man was described to me as someone who "couldn't ever have gotten anybody else. She's lucky she even got him."

Because they look different and because they are resented, the Vietnamese are largely neglected in the life of the community. At this writing, none of the grocery stores in the area handles ingredients specific to Vietnamese cuisine, although the manager of one of them has expressed a casual interest in doing so. The Vietnamese are not numerous enough to support their own church and so attend the regular Catholic church in Henderson. They are not fully welcome in religion classes and the priest has made little effort to hold special masses for them. (Occasionally a Vietnamese priest travels through the area and conducts masses in Vietnamese. He is only marginally welcomed by the regular priest.) Vietnamese are not welcomed at the bars and dance halls of the area, and the community has made no effort to provide facilities for them.

Nor are they accommodated in other respects. Their opinions are not sought on political matters that affect them, and they are forced to depend on intermediaries, such as the local Catholic priest, when they need assistance. Most of the Vietnamese live in two trailer parks within the corporate limits of the town. However, none of them is a citizen, and, accordingly, they cannot vote. As a result, local politics is conducted without regard to their needs. Technically, the Vietnamese could attend city council meetings and voice their opinions, but few of the adults are sufficiently proficient in English or Cajun French to be able to understand the proceedings. Their children, who can understand the language, are too young to understand the complexities of the political system and therefore cannot translate adequately. In general, the Vietnamese comprise a kind of outcast class in the community—welcome for their labor and the money they spend, but not fully included in the activities of the town.

The presence of the Vietnamese is one of the few developments that has caused the local Cajun population to identify as Americans rather than as Cajuns. Generally, when Cajuns refer to someone as an "American," they mean someone who is not Cajun. Cajuns do, of course, acknowledge that they are U.S. citizens. But because they know they are different from the rest of the country, and because in Louisiana they have historically been referred to as "French" because of their language, they refer to themselves as Cajuns or as French. However, when they contrast themselves with their Vietnamese neighbors, they identify as Americans. This is strictly a situational use of the term, implying that the Vietnamese should have fewer rights because they are outsiders and stressing the Cajuns' closer alliance with the rest of the United States than with their Oriental neighbors.

Apart from the Vietnamese, who are only marginal members of the community, social life in Henderson includes members of all personalities, personal convictions, and habits. The kinship ties and the contingencies of small town life require people to accommodate one another's idiosyncrasies as much as possible. In general, there is little in Henderson daily life that inspires genuine controversy—with one major exception. The aspect of life that is most controversial, that inspires the most conflict, and yet is considered a great form of public entertainment, is politics. If on other levels social life is relatively smooth, it is in the political domain that social life is the most dramatic.

7 / Politics

Henderson is a highly political town. Politics there is a sport in which everybody takes an active interest and many participate. On learning of my intent to write a book about the town, many residents immediately inquired whether I was going to write about politics. "That's all there is around here, just politics," was a typical reply. Issues that elsewhere would be simple conflicts become heavily politicized in Henderson, and factional disputes are strong. Some residents are embarrassed about the way in which their local politics are depicted in outside news media, but in general they fully enjoy the spirit of the conflicts and eagerly anticipate the results.

Elections really are treated as a kind of spectator sport. Residents discuss the virtues and the faults of the various candidates for public office as a matter of routine. During the 1983 election for state representative, each of the three candidates campaigned door to door in the Henderson area, leaving brochures at each house. One afternoon I visited the family of old Mr. Holden Serrette, a household that had been solicited by each of the candidates. After dinner (lunch), Mr. Serrette pulled out his pile of political brochures for discussion. The candidates were evaluated according to looks and demeanor, personality where known, and the friends and associates they maintained. Each person present had an opinion as to who might win, but none of the six adults present raised the issue of whom they personally would vote for. (None of the candidates in question was from the Henderson area, though one had extensive ties there. As a result, there was no "favorite son" candidate to claim support.) Several days later, when I visited the Serrettes again, Mr. Serrette once more raised the issue of the elections, with a similar focus on the candidates' personalities and similar speculation on who might win.

Henderson residents themselves perceive that they view politics as sport. The mayor uses a sports metaphor in describing politics in the community. When I asked him why he was endorsing certain candidates for city council in 1984, his response was

it's like a football team. You can work best when you work together. I help the ones who help me, that way we can have a winning team.

In fact, as with football games, the outcomes of elections are frequent subjects for gambling. There are no official odds placed, at least not for local elections, but

71

people place their own bets as they choose. Before the 1983 general election, I sat with a group of men in one of the local restaurants. Two of these men were running for the same local office, and the others were placing bets on the outcome (as it happens, both lost to a third candidate). The discussion at the table was spirited and friendly, with each candidate giving mock campaign speeches to convince the others to vote for him. Although the candidates were present and the subject of the bets was politics, the event resembled any football pool anywhere else in the United States, with members trying to gain support for their favorite teams.

POLITICS AND GOVERNMENT

People in Henderson maintain a strong mistrust of government on any level. Their fiercely independent spirit precludes their placing full confidence in any institution or person, other than a religious one, that represents authority. Government, especially on an extralocal level, is perceived as an infringement of the freedom of individuals. Henderson residents prefer to solve their own problems in their own way. This sentiment has softened somewhat on the state level, largely because of the immense popularity of Cajun governor Edwin Edwards, who served the legal maximum of two consecutive terms from 1972 to 1980, and was subsequently reelected in 1983. A Cajun in the governor's mansion has made Henderson residents feel a bit more trusting of state-level government (rumors in Henderson during the 1983 gubernatorial election were that only one person in town opposed Edwards, although Edwards is not from the Henderson area), but they still prefer to have as little to do with government as possible.

Henderson's dislike of government is manifest on many levels. During the 1980 U.S. census, there was concern among parish census-takers that Henderson residents might refuse to cooperate. Bernard Dupuis, who worked as a census enumerator, acknowledged that large numbers of Henderson area residents did not participate willingly in the census. After he visited those who had failed to respond by the deadline and explained to them that they could not be harmed by providing the information requested, he still was not optimistic about the rate of returns. He explained to me that many people would refuse out of fear, mistrust, or just a general desire to avoid cooperation with the government. (This does not count those who were unable to read the forms. Dupuis's assistance made it possible for anybody who wanted to cooperate to have the forms filled out correctly.) Many believe that promises of confidentiality represent lies on the part of the federal government, attempts to trick people into volunteering information they would otherwise not provide. Government is not to be trusted, no matter what its representatives say.

In addition to their dislike of censuses, Henderson residents object to organized attempts to regulate their activities. Henderson was the only community in St. Martin Parish to resist the establishment of a 2 A.M. curfew on the public serving of alcohol; the objection, as mayor Pat Huval put it, was to the attempt to regulate behavior and not to the idea of a limit on alcohol consumption. When the Henderson city council considered (briefly) raising a local tax to provide extra revenues, one local resident said, "The people I've talked to believe tax is a sin." Parish-level politicians know that tax issues will never pass in Henderson, however small the amount, important the issue, or how much support the issue has elsewhere in the parish. When the school board sought (successfully) a sales tax increase in 1984, one board member declared that he knew they couldn't win in Henderson:

> We just have to hope we can get enough support in other places, because we know we'll lose in Henderson. There's nothing we can do about that. Those people just won't vote for taxes, it doesn't matter what it is.

In fact, the issue did lose in Henderson and in other nearby precincts, though it carried most of the precincts in the parish.

Despite its dislike of government, Henderson is a remarkably political town. The residents fully understand the differences between politics and government, and see no conflict between being intrigued by politics and mistrusting government. Political anthropologists, political scientists, and other students of the political process have long distinguished between government, or the official maintenance of order, and politics, which refers to the manipulation of power. In Henderson, where organized attempts to control behavior are strongly resented, the jockeying for local power is a major activity and source of amusement. When residents say that politics runs the community, they refer to political action as reflected in power plays, coalition building, and local-level adversary action. They do not refer to the trappings of outside government or to the maintenance of order, which they ignore as best they can. This is a distinction not as readily made elsewhere in the United States, where government is more widely trusted and is viewed as the same as politics.

It must be noted that while local citizens mistrust outside government, successful Henderson politicians do not. Quite the contrary: the effective political leaders of the community are highly skilled manipulators of government at all levels from parish to state. The town's mayor has fashioned a political career by manipulating and befriending government officials at all levels. City council and other local elections in Henderson are characterized by the formation of alliances and by public reciprocal endorsements. However, the political issues that arouse popular sentiment in Henderson are usually local in nature and do not involve other levels of government. The alliances politicians form with elected officials on higher levels may aid Henderson, but they are not central to the issues of major public concern. As a result, although local politicians may be admired for their skills in forming alliances and in manipulating other levels of government, citizens as a whole see little use for these alliances and prefer to trust only those local-level politicians whom they know well.

POLITICAL ORGANIZATION OF THE COMMUNITY

The town of Henderson is officially governed by a mayor and a five-member city council. These officials, along with the local chief of police, are elected every four years. Elections are bitter, fierce, and hotly contested, and they form a constant topic of conversation during and long after the election season. To date, although the composition of the council has changed since the town was incorporated in 1971, the only mayor Henderson has ever had is Pat Huval.

Pat Huval became mayor in 1971 as a result of his successful efforts to incorporate the town. His desire to incorporate stemmed from his wish to have Henderson indicated on official maps of Louisiana, with the expectation that his restaurant business would profit if the town were clearly identified on the maps. Because Pat undertook all of the legal proceedings to obtain incorporation, and because of his preexisting alliances with key officials on the state level, he was appointed the town's first mayor in 1971 and elected in the first elections of 1972. Since that year he has won each of the three subsequent mayoral races.

Pat Huval has ensured his popularity within the community through many years of doing personal favors for people in need. He has spent his own funds to pay utility bills for people who could not afford to pay their own; he has fed hungry local families at his restaurants and has allowed homeless people to sleep at his house. Personal favors of this nature are not expected of all politicians as a matter of routine, and Henderson residents know they cannot make similar demands on other elected officials. This is simply Pat's personal style, and it is a style that is much appreciated by his constituents. In a community in which help is expected only of kin, personal favors extended by the mayor are long remembered. This has produced a support base that has never been effectively challenged despite several valiant attempts.

It should be noted that Pat's method of maintaining his constituency strongly resembles the "big man" method employed by many peoples around the world, and for similar reasons. Tribal groups on the big-man level of organization are generally composed of small, self-contained units in which all members are intimately acquainted and usually related. Local-level leaders are needed to ensure adequate distribution of goods, to maintain internal order, and to regulate relations with others. However, because all members of the group are essentially equal, no one individual can claim power by right. As a result, power accrues to the individual who makes himself indispensible to others (big men are virtually always male) by doing favors and making personal sacrifices on behalf of his constituents. A big man has power only because others are willing to give it to him in return for favors and services rendered. When he loses his ability to do favors or provide services for others, a big man usually loses the power to a rival who surpasses him in generosity. In other words, power goes to the man who can best indebt others to him (see Service 1975:72–73).

In Henderson, where political issues are generally local in nature and where egalitarianism has traditionally prevailed, a local-level leader who can maintain his position by doing favors for others may be the most appropriate kind of leader. In fact, like that of a tribal big man, Pat's political popularity has fluctuated with the state of his personal finances. During the 1970s, when he and the town were most prosperous and he could afford to be generous with his own money, Pat's popularity soared. At his political rally in 1980, Pat made a speech describing how much money he possessed and how much he had given to the people of the community. However, he suffered some financial setbacks during the early 1980s, and his generosity toward his constituents suffered of necessity. This occurred at a time when the town itself was experiencing economic hardship, and while there were more people in need, Pat had fewer resources with which to help them. The most successful challenge to Pat's political career came in 1984, when he defeated his opponent by a mere 32 votes. As with a big-man system, the ability to spend money on behalf of constituents is a way to ensure continued influence in Henderson; when that ability declines, so does the power that accompanies it.

This is not to suggest that Pat is uniformly popular. Many Henderson residents dislike him personally, politically, or both. Although everyone will readily admit that Pat has worked and sacrificed to help the town, many believe he now demands too much in return. Some maintain that he will not tolerate disagreement and that he wants to run the town singlehandedly. Still others complain that he is a crook (in fact he has been convicted and pardoned of income tax evasion, a point discussed below). Another complaint, coming largely from better educated residents, is that Pat is not sufficiently educated (he is proud that he had only four years of schooling) or sophisticated to run a government. Some of Pat's opponents express their dissatisfaction both verbally and at the polls as well as in their business transactions. Others complain, particularly about the extent of the allegiance they owe him, and vote for him anyway. That he received only 58 percent of the vote in 1980 and 52 percent in 1984 demonstrates that Pat's control is not as great as it may appear.

For several years Pat and the chief of police have been serious political rivals. The two were allied during the early years of incorporation and ran together in the 1976 elections. However, by 1980 they were bitterly opposed, and their conflicts have been reflected in elections and in the political processes of the town ever since.

In large part, the rivalry concerns the allocation of scarce town funds. The mayor maintains that the chief uses too much money for his department and that other city services are underfunded as a result. The chief, for his part, claims that he knows what is necessary to run a police force and that the mayor is simply unwilling to provide adequate police protection for the community. Some Henderson residents are personally allied with the chief, who is also in a position to do favors for people (he can overlook minor violations of the law, for example). These people may oppose Pat if their loyalty to the chief is sufficiently high, though they need not. As a result of this conflict between two otherwise popular community leaders, election results can be highly polarized.

POLITICAL ALLIANCES AND OBLIGATIONS

The standard method of running for elected office in the Henderson area is to form tickets or slates of candidates. Candidates running for different offices during the same election will team up with the intent of garnering support for one another. This holds true not just in the strictly local mayoral and council elections, but also in elections for parish and even state-level positions. For example, during the statewide elections in 1983, candidates for police jury (county commissioner)

Pat Huval's 1984 campaign headquarters. The Texaco station is currently out of business but at one time was owned by Pat. Note the list of candidates running on Pat's ticket.

and state representative teamed up and bought joint ads in the local newspaper. Likewise, during the local council and mayoral election in 1984, Pat Huval promoted a ticket headed by himself and including one candidate for chief of police and three for the city council.

However, in recent years the political ticket has been less effective than it was in the past. At one time area residents were not sufficiently educated to evaluate candidates objectively and could be more easily coerced into voting for a slate of candidates than they can today. The general consensus among Henderson residents, expressed to me by several older citizens, is that "people are smarter now than they used to be" and are in a better position to make independent evaluations of the candidates. In any case, the independent spirit of the people of Henderson acts against political tickets because residents like to think they are voting according to their own wishes and not according to the dictates of some politician. Today, slates in the area are not always elected in full. Running on the ticket of even a popular incumbent is no longer a guarantee of victory because each candidate is voted for independently and a vote for one member of a ticket has no effect on the others. In 1980 only two of Pat's four endorsed council candidates won, and all of the police chief candidates he has endorsed since his fight with the incumbent have lost. In fact, in 1984 the incumbent chief, strongly opposed by Pat, won a resounding victory despite Pat's lesser victory. In 1984 two of Pat's three endorsed council candidates won—better than in 1980, but still not enough to guarantee him a majority on the five-member council. The plea for "teamwork" and Pat's slogan "Give me a team I can work with" had only a minor effect on the voters, many of whom insisted on voting independently regardless of endorsements and slate membership.

In fact, many political candidates in Henderson now run expressly as "independents." This designation has nothing to do with political party membership, as it does in national elections in the United States. (All candidates in Henderson have always been registered as Democrats. National party politics play no part in local elections.) Rather, an independent in Henderson is someone who is not beholden to anyone else or officially running on anybody else's ticket. In Henderson, the designation "independent" is often a veiled reference to Pat, who controls the political tickets; it means the candidate is not expressly allied with him. As a result, Pat often campaigns vigorously against independent candidates, claiming that "independence" is a euphemism for opposition to him and his policies. Independent candidates have run remarkably well in local city council elections; in 1984 three of the five elected council members ran as independents.

For all of its effectiveness, independent voting occurs only on a very local level. Despite their claims of independence, many Henderson residents vote for higher-level (parish and state) candidates according to the tickets endorsed by their local leaders. Pat has long been an avid supporter of Governor Edwards (Edwards's political memorabilia are prominently displayed at his restaurant, and Edwards was the featured guest speaker at Pat's mayoral fundraiser held in 1984), and in the 1983 election Edwards won resoundingly in the Henderson area. Edwards's local victory was attributable partially to his Cajun heritage, but also to the confidence of Henderson residents that he would work for them because he had the support of their mayor. The candidate Pat endorsed for police juror in 1983 was elected as well. Because residents so mistrust higher levels of government, they tend to vote for the person they have reason to think might best look after their interests, and this is usually the person endorsed by their leader. They recognize the importance of the obligations attendant to political endorsements, and while they resent being beholden on a local level, they are eager to gain the assistance of higher-level officials who otherwise might take advantage of them.

Running on a ticket does indeed obligate a candidate to the head of the ticket. Pat expects those he endorses to support his policies and to vote his way at council meetings. Candidates Pat helped elect who subsequently fail to support some of his policies find themselves the targets of vigorous and vicious campaigns to unseat them. Likewise, when Pat endorses a candidate for a higher office, he expects that in return for his support that official will work on behalf of Henderson. Consequently, especially on a local level, candidates must evaluate carefully whether to run with Pat. Prior to 1984, when there were multiple issues at stake in the local mayoral election, this was potentially a delicate decision, because a candidate might have supported Pat on some issues and opposed him on others. For various reasons, the 1984 election centered around a single issue: the conflict between the mayor and the chief of police. As a result, issues were more clear-cut, and the decision to join Pat's ticket or to remain independent was relatively easier.

Political battles in Henderson are generally highly polarized: in favor of and opposed to Pat Huval. Candidates or voters who publicly commit themselves to one of these positions inherit a series of obligations beyond who to vote for and which positions to support. Basic details of daily life such as which restaurant to eat at or where a person can work can be determined by political alliances. One man complained that he is restricted in where he can go in town because he is on bad terms with both the police chief and the mayor, each of whom owns a restaurant and has strong allies in other parts of the community:

> I went to [the mayor's restaurant] the other day and everybody looked at me like I was the enemy or something. All I wanted was to sit and eat and mind my own business, and they ran me out of there because I'm not one of their crowd. And the last time I went to [the chief's restaurant] he told me to meet him on the levee [a challenge to fight], so I can't go there anymore either. You can't just mind your own business around here.

Likewise, after the 1984 election, when Pat barely defeated his opponent, his ex-wife Agnes was extremely upset about how badly he had done. She strongly supported Pat, despite their divorce, because

> I was with him when he gave his own money to start this town. That was my money too, and my kids'. Those people who didn't vote for him, I don't know how they can forget what we did to help them and this town.

The day after the election she told me she was not going to hire people to work at her restaurant unless she had reason to think they had supported Pat. She saw no reason to help people who couldn't appreciate what he had done for them: "I'll just hire people from [the community where she grew up], or the ones that I know well. I'm not going to have those other people working for me."

In Henderson as elsewhere, political and personal favors are routinely granted to supporters. Jobs, both for the town and in private business, can be given to supporters and can be taken away if support lags. After the election of 1984, one of the unsuccessful police chief candidates found himself out of work and with no political office forthcoming. Because he had run against the incumbent chief, he was able to approach Pat for help in setting up a business on some of Pat's property. It was possible for him to make this request only because he had helped in trying to unseat the mayor's rival. A similar arrangement would not have been considered with a person with the "wrong" political connections.

The obligation to vote for somebody who has helped you in part explains why both the chief and the mayor continue to be reelected despite their intense conflict. Although most town residents recognize the community's debt to Pat, many are also indebted to the chief for one reason or another. The chief can, for example, ignore minor violations of the 2 A.M. curfew, permitting local bar and restaurant owners to make a little more money. He can fail to arrest local citizens for fighting, drunk driving, or other minor offenses, or he can reduce the charges against them. He also does personal favors for residents, such as checking the security of their houses and barns. As a result, many voters are indebted to both of the political rivals and find it impossible to vote a straight ticket.

The exchange of favors for votes holds true not just on the local level but on higher levels as well. One fisher who had been a strong supporter of the successful candidate for state representative in 1983 admitted that he hoped for a job as game warden in return for his support. A policeman in a town near Henderson told me he was supporting a particular candidate in the local sheriff's election because he had reason to believe that candidate might appoint him as a deputy. He told me explicitly that "You vote for the one who can best help you."

Often in Henderson "the one who can best help you" is a relative. Because of the nature of kinship obligations, a close relative in political office may be expected to aid kin with whatever benefits are available. The chief of police has hired his wife, a brother, and several other family members to work for the police department, at one time relinquishing a part of his own salary to help pay that of his brother. Pat Huval's wife works as the town clerk. The granddaughter of one of the council members is employed in a city job. These are the kinds of benefits that politicians can and do give to kin in return for loyalty and support. It is expected that officials will try to help their relatives, though not to excess (the chief is sometimes criticized for hiring too many of his family members to work for him). However, beneficiaries of political favors are expected to remain supportive of the official and know that they may lose the position if their support wavers.

Although officials are generally expected to aid their own family members in return for support, people are not necessarily expected to vote for or support their relatives in political endeavors. Most people do vote for close relatives as a matter of course. In 1983 Pat Huval and his wife each supported a different candidate for police juror because one was his cousin and the other was her uncle. "Naturally family comes first," they wrote in a paid political ad, and "each voted for their relative." However, candidates cannot always count on the support of kin, especially distant kin. This is consistent with the general pattern of kinship obligations in Henderson: one is expected to aid close kin but may use discretion with more distant kin. And in a town like Henderson a given voter may be related to more than one candidate for the same position. In 1983 two men who described themselves as second cousins ran for the same police jury seat; obviously their shared relatives were forced to make a choice. Candidates routinely appeal to voters on the basis of kinship, but they understand that they may not be able to count on the support. For example, Bernard Dupuis maintains that he won't vote for somebody just because they're related to him:

> I don't care if they're my cousin or something. If I don't want you there I won't vote for you. You can be the best person in the world and not be right for the job, and if I don't think you can do the job I won't vote for you.

One elderly woman explained that she would not vote for one of her relatives in an upcoming election because she didn't think he was smart enough to handle the job:

> He's nice, he's always been good to me, but I don't think he's got what it takes for politics. I just can't see him in that job. I'm not going to vote for him because I think it's wrong for him to be there even though he is my family.

Opinions on this subject are mixed, however. Another older woman explained that she would always vote for a relative in an election "because you have to help your people out. If you can't count on your family there's nothing left."

POLITICAL ISSUES AND CAMPAIGNS

The style of political campaigns in Henderson has varied somewhat over the years, but in general local campaigns are bitter and prolonged. In a community in which people know one another so well, personalities inevitably become variables in the election process, and candidates make frequent reference to one another's personal backgrounds. Although issues are raised, issues and personalities often become mixed into a single attack. In fact, in many instances the issues are truly not separable from the personalities of the candidates.

Politics in Henderson revolves around a small number of key issues. The key issue generally concerns budgetary matters, which have increased in importance as the town's revenues have fallen. The economic slump that began in the early 1980s left Henderson with a diminished sales tax base, in part because many residents were out of work and had less money to spend, and in part because of the related decline in the restaurant business. This caused severe financial problems for the town, which relies heavily on sales taxes for its revenues. At one point the town was forced to lay off almost half of its employees because it could no longer afford to pay their salaries. Huval is determined not to permit the town to borrow money (one of the accomplishments of which he is most proud is that Henderson has never been in debt to anyone) and he will cut spending wherever possible before he accepts a loan. His opponents claim that it is entirely reasonable for a municipality to borrow money when necessary, and that cutting spending can place the community at great risk if needed services are eliminated. This debate, or variations thereof, has dominated campaign issues since Henderson was incorporated.

Budgetary matters are important concerns and are taken seriously by the residents of the town. In characteristic Henderson style, though, they are addressed through personal attacks on the candidates. In 1980 mayoral candidate James Patin accused Huval of being an inefficient manager and ran on a platform of efficient, honest government. Huval had suggested raising certain local taxes, and Patin claimed that the existing tax base would be sufficient if sales taxes were accurately reported and if somebody with a good education were in charge. However, Patin did not restrict his campaigning to public issues; he placed ads stating that Huval had "run both his and the town's finances into the ground." This injected a personal element into an important public issue.

The tax argument was repeated in 1984, when the major campaign issues concerned the operation of the police department radio room. Huval wanted to replace the radio room with a beeper system, which would be less expensive because it would require considerably fewer personnel. The chief claimed that beepers would be inadequate, however inexpensive they may be. During the 1984 campaign, Huval accused the chief of wanting to keep the radio room because he employed several of his relatives there, and also accused council members sympathetic with the chief of pandering to a special interest and of being incapable of seeing the true needs of the town. The chief and his supporters, in turn, accused Pat of having no concern for or understanding of law enforcement, of vindictiveness, and of not enforcing tax collection which, they claimed, would alleviate the town's budget problems and permit the radio room to operate. Although the real issue was the radio room, the arguments were couched in terms of the personalities and motives of the principals.

Some Henderson politicians are surrounded by considerable public scandal. Pat Huval was convicted in 1978 of income tax evasion, though he was subsequently pardoned by Governor Edwards. Few residents are sympathetic with the IRS, and many respect a person who can successfully circumvent governmental regulations. Nonetheless, this conviction has branded Huval a "crook" in the eyes of some of his constituents and has provided a weapon for opponents. (This issue was a major one during the 1980 mayoral election, which occurred shortly after the conviction and pardon took place. By 1984 it was forgotten and was not raised at all during the campaign.) The chief of police has also been involved in two controversies of greater local import: a shooting, in which his brother (a policeman on duty) was a victim, and the false arrest of a citizen (the mother of the man convicted of shooting the chief's brother) who filed an expensive lawsuit that the city was forced to pay for. As a result of these issues, it has been relatively easy for candidates to rely on personal attacks in their campaigns and to turn these into major campaign issues.

In 1980 personal insults were traded hard and fast among the mayoral candidates. Although this is a common occurrence, it was facilitated in that year by the recency of both Huval's and the chief's personal scandals. For example, mayoral candidate James Patin placed an ad in the local paper which read, in part, "Every other state and parish in the United States forbids anyone convicted of a felony to vote or run for public office . . . why doesn't the law apply here?" This ad contained no mention of Patin's qualifications, but rather a lengthy discussion of Huval's income tax conviction. Huval's response was to run an ad featuring his letter of pardon—which had absolved him of guilt and restored his full rights—and to state that he would rather spend his money helping the people of Henderson than pay the IRS. At a political rally just before the election, Huval repeated that he prefers to spend his money on his people rather than to give it to the government. This defense capitalized on the favors Pat had done for his constituents as well as on his constituents' mistrust of government. In the end, Patin's attack had little effect. Nonetheless, it was considered a legitimate campaign issue and was raised with much public fanfare.

Huval, in turn, raised personal attacks against Patin. Patin is known around town for employing large numbers of Vietnamese workers in his seafood plant. He has been instrumental in helping his Vietnamese workers become established in Henderson, and many Cajun residents resent him for it. At his rally in 1980, Huval and one of the councilmen running on his ticket each made a speech exhorting citizens not to vote for Patin, lest the town be overrun by Vietnamese. Huval told the crowd that if they elected Patin, "before you know it this town will have more Vietnamese than voters." This was not an election issue, and it addressed none of the issues of efficiency that Patin had raised during his campaign. But, like Patin's accusations against Pat, this was raised to cast aspersions on the opponent's character. It had the desired effect.

Also in 1980, Pat waged a public debate with a councilman he opposed. Huval and the councilman in question placed ads side by side in the newspaper, accusing one another of lying, of trying to protect special interests, and of working for selfish rather than public ends. The councilman claimed that Pat was vindictive, arbitrary, and was trying to bully his constituents. Pat's ad referred to the councilman as a "two-faced liar," claiming that the charges leveled against him were false. In response, the councilman erected a large sign in front of his place of

1980 campaign sign.

business: "PAT HUVAL YOU'RE A TRIPLE FACE LIER" [sic]. The councilman was not reelected.

Campaigning in Henderson is by no means restricted to the public trading of insults. In a small community it is imperative to make personal contact with as many voters as possible. Candidates routinely travel from house to house during their campaigns. It is very important to visit all residences in town lest a voter be insulted. Huval's only opponent in 1984 ran an ad in the weekly paper just prior to the election asking for support and apologizing in case he had omitted visiting anybody. "I want to thank the people of Henderson for their warm welcome as I went house to house as a political candidate. . . . If I missed anyone, I'm sorry. I mean well, and I have the best interest of our community at heart." Incumbents and better known candidates may simply shake hands, exchange friendly greetings, and ask for the personal favor of a vote. Lesser known candidates must spend more time visiting with voters, trying to convince them to risk voting for someone not currently in office. In these cases kin ties are frequently brought up: a candidate may remind a voter of a distant kin tie, hoping (but not necessarily expecting) that this relationship will yield additional votes.

Candidates for all offices produce small flyers that they distribute during their house-to-house visits and leave, in stacks, at area businesses. These flyers have a standard format and are virtually identical in appearance. They are 3 inches wide and 6 inches long, printed on white cover stock paper. Each features a black-and-white photograph of the candidate on the front, with the candidate's name and the office sought. The back contains the candidate's name and desired office, followed by a list of qualifications and a plea for support. Qualifications generally include the names of the candidate's wife and children, educational background (especially if the candidate is a graduate of the local high school), length of residence in Henderson, and occupation. This section is generally followed by a brief campaign statement, most often pledging to work for the unity and harmony of the town.

In addition to the flyers and the house-to-house campaigns, candidates try to hold public rallies to generate support. This is not always possible for candidates for city council, especially for those running as independents, because such a party is expensive. Candidates for higher-level offices such as police juror or state representative are frequently able to hold parties of this sort, as is Pat Huval for himself and for those he supports. There are two types of political parties: a rally to generate support and a fundraiser. The principal difference is that a rally is free and open to the public, while a fundraiser has an admission fee that can run as high as $50 per couple. Otherwise, the two events are similar. They feature local bands and dancing, free beer and food, and short but rousing speeches by the candidates, by supporters, and sometimes by special guests (often Governor Edwards).

Both rallies and fundraisers are popular in Henderson and are generally well attended. In fact, the difference between the two is less profound than it may appear, because not all guests at the fundraisers pay the full admission price. Few residents of Henderson are willing to spend $50 for a party, no matter how much "free" beer they can drink. When Pat held a $50-per-couple fundraiser for his 1984 mayoral campaign (featuring Governor Edwards as a guest speaker), free tickets were distributed to loyal followers and close friends. This was common knowledge around town, so that most of Pat's supporters who wanted to attend were able to attend for free. In 1979 I attended a $25-per-couple fundraiser for a candidate for state representative. The hall in which the event was held, capable of holding several hundred people, was full. However, none of the people I questioned had paid; all said they were there because they had been given free tickets. One woman explained to me that

> he [the candidate] couldn't ever sell all those tickets at $25. Nobody would pay that. So he gives them away. Or maybe a big supporter donates a lot of money to the campaign and he gives them a lot of tickets, and they give them away. That way people have a good time, which makes them like him, and it makes it look like he has a lot of support, which makes other people want to vote for him. If the place is crowded it makes the ones who did pay feel better about it. So everybody is better off if he just gives away all those extra tickets that he couldn't sell.

Even at the fundraisers, then, the purpose is to fill the hall with supporters and to generate excitement over the election and for the candidate in question.

Candidates in the Henderson area know that if they have a good band and good food they will attract a large crowd. Many residents freely admit that they attend political parties simply for the "good time," for the food, the beer, and the dancing. Many even attend rallies for candidates they oppose, simply for the entertainment. During the 1983 governor's race, Edwards's opponent held a large rally near Henderson. This candidate had very little local support, but he had a large turnout at his rally. Several confirmed Edwards supporters of my acquaintance went, they said, because they wanted to "drink his [the opponent's] beer and dance to his band."

An important feature of these parties, aside from the free food, drink, and music, are the testimonials given by invited guests and local citizens. This is especially important because many attendees are there simply for the entertainment and may need to be convinced to support the candidate staging the party. The testimonials are held after the band has been playing for a while but before the food is served, which guarantees a captive audience: none of the guests will leave before the food is served. The speeches are generally short, lest they be considered boring, and are designed to make voters believe they will be personally served by electing the candidate in question.

At his 1980 rally, Pat called several elderly Henderson residents to the bandstand, each of whom recounted a tale of misfortune that Pat had personally helped solve. In most of these cases Pat's assistance had been in the form of a personal loan or cash payment, and he had operated as an individual rather than within the official duties of mayor. (One case involved garbage collection, and the solution to the problem was a legitimate exercise of mayoral duties.) This pattern was repeated at the 1984 rally, at which citizens spoke about Pat's generosity, concern for the town, and ability to get things done.

The rallies and the newspaper ads are the aspects of politics that Henderson residents most enjoy. The public trading of insults, the charges and counter-charges, and the anticipation of an opponent's reaction are what make politics exciting. These activities generate the most public discussion for the longest period of time. Politics as sport is best seen in these campaign ads and parties: voters discuss the arguments and debates over and over, rehashing each step as they would the plays in a football game. While political outcomes may have important implications for the lives of the citizens, politics is truly enjoyed for its entertainment value, regardless of the outcome of individual elections.

POLITICS AND ETHNIC IDENTITY

Many observers of ethnic groups have discussed the role that ethnic identity plays in politics. It is frequently noted that ethnic issues become political issues when the culture of the group is threatened. In such an instance, local politicians will use their ethnic identity to gain power and will build platforms based on ethnic issues to help protect and preserve the heritage of their constituents.

In Henderson this has not occurred—nor, for that matter, has this happened anywhere else in the Cajun area. Ethnic identity in Henderson cannot be considered, in any meaningful sense, a political issue. Campaigns have never been waged on ethnic platforms, and no candidate for any public office in the history of the community has ever used ethnic identity as an issue. (Governor Edwin Edwards is a notable exception. He is a skilled master of ethnic politics and has helped to ensure his popularity with Cajun voters by emphasizing his own Cajun background. However, his appeal to ethnic identity is designed to make voters trust him; he does not raise issues of cultural persistence or preservation in his appeals for the Cajun vote. Also, he is not a local candidate, nor is his a local office.) Issues of ethnic identity are simply not of major concern to the voters of Henderson, at least not on a political level.

Instead, the crucial issue in Henderson politics is the distinction between insiders and outsiders. For example, it is expected that all local public officials will be Cajun. The overwhelming majority of Henderson voters are Cajun, of course (the Vietnamese, not being citizens, cannot vote), and they can and do elect their own. Public officials are expected to be long-term residents of the community, and this almost by definition excludes non-Cajuns from consideration. A "stranger," someone relatively unfamiliar with the community and without extensive kin ties there, will find it virtually impossible to get elected to anything. While several Cajun residents are perceived as "strangers" because they have not lived in Henderson for very long, virtually all of the non-Cajun residents are seen as "strangers" as well. These people cannot be elected to public office. In 1984 one candidate for police chief had lived in Henderson for only seven years; he fared the worst of the three candidates, taking only 9 percent of the vote. One long-time resident explained that this candidate had done poorly "because people don't really know him, who his family is. They don't know whether they can trust him."

Although successful candidates must be insiders, it is not necessary for a candidate to have been born in Henderson: not even Pat Huval can make that claim. Candidates do, however, list the length of their residence in Henderson among their qualifications for public office. "Lived in Henderson for 22 years," "resident of Henderson for 23 years," "resident of Henderson since 1973," and similar claims are routine components of campaign literature. While these statements are not explicitly designed to keep non-Cajuns out of office, they do serve to indicate a person who may not be sufficiently local or sufficiently Cajun to hold public office. One of the 1976 mayoral candidates told me explicitly that he had run "to look after our people and protect them from outsiders." This was brought home during an area election for judge in 1984. The incumbent, a Cajun from another parish, had the reputation of being dishonest, hot-tempered, and unfair; his opponent, widely recognized as capable and level-headed, was an Anglo from northern Louisiana. The campaign focused almost exclusively on these differences. The incumbent ran ads claiming to be "one of us" and maintaining that only a person who shared Cajun heritage could serve the area adequately. The opponent addressed the controversial nature of the incumbent's character, claiming that "he's *not* one of us" (because no good Cajun would do the things alleged). In a close election the incumbent won.

The importance of the distinction between insiders and outsiders cannot be overestimated. There is a strong feeling in Henderson that "we can take care of our own." During one of the most heated political conflicts in the town's history, this subject was made very clear. In 1978 a policeman, the brother of the chief, was shot in the line of duty. Another officer was killed, and a private citizen was arrested and subsequently jailed for the incident. The man convicted was engaged in a personal feud with the family of the chief, and especially of the chief's brother. The subject of this feud was raised as an issue during city council discussions of the incident. The entire controversy was highly publicized and occupied several city council meetings. However, the feelings of citizens in town was that "outsiders" (reporters) were responsible for the publicity and that the families involved could resolve the personal aspect of this problem by themselves if "outsiders" would only let them.

There is, however, an ethnic component to politics in the Henderson area that is subtle and transcends the issues and debates that comprise the management of government. In general, English is the language of politics in Henderson. City council meetings are conducted in English, and most campaign speeches are delivered in that language as well. This is because politics, by definition, is a public domain. City council meetings are open to the public and to the press, and must therefore be conducted in the language deemed appropriate for events subject to public scrutiny.

However, in certain contexts French can be used for explicitly political ends. Because candidates must be perceived as Cajun with a genuine understanding of the needs of the people, French can be a valuable political tool. Political rallies are officially conducted in English, but candidates frequently open their speeches with a few sentences in French to establish themselves as trustworthy. During the controversial 1984 area judgeship race, the Cajun incumbent used French in his printed ads and in his speeches, knowing that his opponent could not do the same. Pat routinely mixes French with English in his public speeches, as does Governor Edwards. This reminds constituents that the candidate is one of them, that he understands and can communicate effectively with them.

Use of French in politics goes beyond the public use at rallies. Deals and private negotiations are generally conducted in French, and private conversations among council members preceding the meetings, at which political matters are often discussed, are held in French. During council meetings, members may mutter asides to one another in French, particularly if they are angry. The contrast between the private use of French outside the formal context of public meetings and rallies, and the public use of English within these formal domains, suggests that Henderson residents perceive politics as a public enactment of what are ultimately private matters.

As time passes, French will become increasingly less important in the political arena in Henderson. City council members are now being chosen from among the young members of the community, not all of whom are conversant in French. Young people do not find it important that their candidates speak French, and within a generation or so it will no longer matter whether a councilman or the mayor can speak to his constituents in French. What will continue to be important, however, is the preservation of the way of life that Henderson residents cherish. This is closely linked with cultural patterns that do not necessarily include the

French language but that remain important to the younger generation. In 1984 a 30-year-old Henderson native ran for city council, stating his purpose as follows:

> I see a duty in all of us to help mold a future not only for ourselves but for our children. After all, we have the same goal in life—to provide them with the same kind of life we have enjoyed since we were kids.

What matters, then, is the perpetuation of a way of life associated not with ethnic identity but with culture. In Henderson, where traditional Cajun culture has been making a relatively smooth accommodation to outside pressures, ethnic matters are singularly unimportant in local politics. Henderson residents think of themselves as Henderson residents first, and Cajuns second. Traditionally self-reliant and independent, they prefer to remain that way and this is expressed through their political behavior as well as through other things they do. What they want is to continue to do things their own way, without the meddlesome interference of "outsiders." They handle things themselves, in their own language (whatever that may be). This implies a perpetuation of certain valued culture traits, but more than anything it suggests an indifference to the politicization of ethnic concerns. In Henderson as elsewhere in the region, Cajun identity is manipulated as a political tool, but it is not an issue. Because it is not truly threatened in Henderson, Cajun culture survives here without recourse to ethnic politics.

8/Making a living

Cajuns take great pride in working hard. They consider themselves to be people who "work hard and play hard," and to describe someone as "not afraid to work" is high praise. Obituary columns in the local newspaper eulogize leading citizens as "a hard worker who will be missed." Cajuns' folk history—their accounts of their own past—includes the hardships the early Acadian settlers faced in trying to carve out a new life in Louisiana. Work, then, is integral to the Cajun self-image.

Cajuns do indeed work hard. From farming and fishing to oil rig work and related enterprises, most Cajuns have always been manual laborers with physically difficult jobs. The traditional lack of education made many other kinds of work inaccessible. Because the economy was slow and the area underdeveloped until recently, few opportunities were available locally for those who were able to obtain educations.

Today Cajuns have ample opportunities to work at white-collar professions close to home, and hard work need not necessarily entail manual labor. However, with the exceptions of the teaching profession and the ownership of small local businesses, most white-collar jobs are located in Lafayette, the business capital of the region. Many people who work in Lafayette live in outlying areas, but many of the residents of the small towns continue to work at more traditional kinds of manual occupations. This is especially true in Henderson, with its heavy fishing base. As a result, although Cajuns are by no means all manual laborers today, those in the smaller rural communities tend to remain blue-collar workers.

ATTITUDES TOWARD WORK

As much as Cajuns take pride in working hard, work itself is generally deemed unpleasant. The mystique of the Cajun as a hard worker is derived directly from the predominance of manual labor, which is deemed arduous and unpleasant work. The attitude has carried over to other types of occupations as well, including those that are less physically demanding. This mystique applies especially to men, who have always been the principal supporters of their families. Now that so many

89

women are employed, they have accepted the mystique of hard work even though their occupations are generally less physically arduous than those of men. Women work as teachers, hairdressers, secretaries, sales clerks, crawfish peelers, or waitresses, or they remain homemakers. Nonetheless, women, as well as men with office jobs, have adopted the notion of themselves as hard workers and take pride in being able to work long hours at difficult and unpleasant tasks.

The idea that work is necessary but unpleasant, done because there is no choice but not valued for its own sake, differs markedly from the Protestant work ethic that prevails in other parts of the United States. Work to a Cajun is neither a virtue nor an end in itself, nor is it something that one should want to do. It is a necessary evil, a means to an end, a way to stay alive (and, today, to afford the luxuries that money can buy). It is not expected that one will like one's job—in fact, one is expected to complain about working. Cajuns regularly complain about how hard they have to work and how nice it would be not to have to work at all. "Travailler c'est trop dur" (Working is too hard) is the title of a popular Cajun song, and the attitude prevails in life as well as in music.

These attitudes hold true in Henderson as much as in any other Cajun community. Residents, with their recent history of self-sufficiency and near poverty, are very proud of having brought themselves into modern prosperity through hard work. They are also aware that, no matter how hard they may work today, things were much more difficult for their ancestors of even one generation ago. Percy Serrette, himself a hard worker and something of a hustler for his own business, describes his father Holden as follows:

> He really had to work hard. They had to do everything for themselves in those days. No tractors, no power tools. Everything was done the hard way. And mom, she worked hard too. Cleaning up after all of us, no washing machine, just an old wood stove. They really had things rough.

But like other Cajuns, while Henderson residents admire a hard worker, they envy and admire someone who has enough money not to have to work. They find it difficult to understand the notion of working for pleasure or of taking pleasure in work. (There is, however, considerable overlap between hobbies and occupations, a point discussed at greater length in Chapter 9.)

Because work is simply a necessary evil, what one does for a living is of little consequence. It is expected that people will switch occupations according to need or desire, and there is no stigma attached to those who change jobs frequently as long as they continue to support themselves. Although elsewhere in the United States an educated person may prefer to remain in a chosen field however poor the pay, a Cajun would consider such a person foolish. During the peak of the oil boom, it was not uncommon for male teachers to quit their jobs and work offshore for an oil company where the pay was better. Female teachers quit to become waitresses, where they earn high tips. Others take part-time jobs in restaurants or in sales to supplement their incomes. The notion of a career ladder, in which the goal is to work hard from the bottom rungs in order to reach the top, is not part of the Cajun philosophy of work. With the possible exception of the professions of medicine and the clergy, Cajuns do not scale their occupations in a prestige hierarchy, and one is free to pick and choose one's occupation.

Cajuns are remarkably flexible in what they can do. This is true especially for men, who learn a variety of skills as children. Most men in the Henderson area have basic electrical and plumbing skills and are at least partially able to perform basic construction tasks. Many build their own homes and are also skilled mechanics. As a result, it is relatively easy for a man, especially a young man, to switch occupations regularly. In 1980 I met Tommy Huval, a young man about 20 years old, who was working as a carpenter's assistant. Six months later he was working as a commercial fisher because he said fishing gave him more independence and the potential to earn more money. After a few months he quit fishing to work as a mechanic, but he still fished on the side to earn extra cash.

This kind of resourcefulness and flexibility is a vestige of age-old Cajun self-sufficiency, which required people to handle most of their own needs. In the past, the ability to perform a number of jobs was a crucial aid to survival. Arcade Calais, now 75 years old, describes his career as one of diverse occupations:

I was raised on the river. I fished some, I worked for the railroad, I did lots of things. Then when the Depression hit I moved to a farm. I never did that before, but I figured if I could just grow a little bit I'd be able to survive. At least I wouldn't starve. After that I worked engineer for a riverboat for a while. You had to do a lot of things to make a living in those days.

Although these conditions and the need for self-sufficiency no longer exist, people in the Henderson area still prefer not to become dependent on others any more than necessary. The accumulation of multiple skills makes it possible for people to remain independent and still earn a living. It also permits a wide choice in occupational strategies and allows a return to a kind of self-sufficiency when necessary. As a result, the accumulation of skills is highly valued in Henderson, and residents view with a combination of pity and scorn a man who cannot perform basic mechanical or repair work for himself and who is forced to depend on others.

This flexibility has served Henderson well in recent years. When the oil industry suffered a decline in the early 1980s, many area men were laid off their jobs. Many went to work as fishers, either for their sole means of support or to supplement the unemployment compensation they were receiving. Others opened small businesses such as welding shops or went into the construction business. In one way or another, most managed to make a successful transition without the kind of hardships experienced by laid off workers in other parts of the United States. This was possible only because of the accumulation of multiple skills and the flexibility concerning work.

Another result of the independent spirit of the people is the high value placed on self-employment. People in the Henderson area dislike being beholden to an employer or a boss and resent having to take orders from somebody else. As a result, they will work for themselves whenever possible. Fishers, as discussed in Chapter 3, are technically self-employed, and by demanding cash payment on delivery they can remain independent of the processors to whom they sell. This is one reason why fishing is such a popular occupation. Some men in the area work as free-lance laborers, performing odd jobs for anybody who will pay. These jobs can range from making local deliveries or pickups to performing basic maintenance or construction chores. Although they contract with others for their work, these people are technically independent workers with no long-term obligations to a single employer. Those men who have gone to work for others, either in the oil fields or in other occupations, complain about having to take orders—and sometimes cannot function in such jobs because of their inability to take orders. One young man was fired from three welding jobs in six months because he refused to obey orders he didn't like. Many men work for wages for a while and eventually open up their own businesses when they have acquired the experience and the contacts to succeed, or after they have retired with a pension from another job and can afford to take the risks of self-employment. Generally speaking, men in the Henderson area will work for others only when they have little choice and will attempt to become independent as soon as they can.

This attitude applies to men more than to women, who traditionally have worked for others. Few women in the area are self-employed, although there are some notable exceptions. Of the women who do work for themselves, many are part-time sales agents for national home sales companies, or do other part-time work out of their homes. Almost half (47 percent) of the Henderson women who were employed in 1979 worked part time (U.S. Census, 1980). This kind of work is preferred by women with small children who need extra money but who do not want to take a full-time job or even a part-time job that requires them to work regular hours. For those women who do choose to work full time, most work for wages for others. Many claim they would prefer the independence of self-employment but are unable to commit the time, energy, and financial resources to running their own business. For women, self-employment and independence remain ideals only sometimes achieved, while for men they are goals to be reached.

In recent years Henderson residents, like other Cajuns, have altered their attitudes toward work. In the past, when anything more than bare subsistence was viewed as prosperity, people were motivated by survival skills rather than by wealth. Work was necessary to ensure survival; people may have worked hard, but the goal was to get by and not to get rich. Today, when wealth is now achievable, many area residents have become interested in accumulating as much as possible. This is mostly an attitude of younger people, the first generation to see the possibility of escaping self-sufficient poverty and of gaining a measure of wealth. For example, Paul Benoit reported that his goal is to be able to borrow a million dollars because that will mean he has been successful enough to have the power of real wealth. Older residents, even those with access to and the opportunity to accumulate a measure of prosperity, still generally prefer comfort to wealth and would rather live more modestly and enjoy themselves than live extravagantly and worry about money. Most of the people with the goal of accumulating wealth are self-employed, and many have several business concerns at the same time.

Although the concern for wealth is relatively new in the Henderson area, and although it may resemble attitudes of U.S. citizens elsewhere, the attitudes behind this concern are still distinctively Cajun. Benoit, for example, is a young man who wants to get rich but who does not enjoy working and does not want to work for an employer even for a high salary. He wants to make his money independently, without having to take orders from somebody else. James Calais, another Henderson resident whose principal topic of conversation is the amount of money he makes at his various business deals, admits that the reason he wants to have a lot of money is

> so that you don't have to take no shit from nobody. If you've got money you can do what you want and you can always take care of yourself.

For many, the concern for wealth is a reaction to the history of poverty: wealth is insurance that you will not have to revert to poverty, self-sufficiency, and deprivation. Even those most motivated by wealth will rarely follow a job to another location; they would rather stay home and find another job, or open their own business, than transfer away from the area no matter how high the pay. The differences between these people and their peers less concerned with money for its own sake is not as great as it might seem; rather than being a basic difference in philosophy, it is a difference in how much is considered enough.

In general, then, the attitude toward work is that it is done in order to survive, it is usually unpleasant, and it is not to be taken too seriously. For some work is a way to get rich (in itself insurance against poverty); for others it is a way to provide the bare necessities and to permit a greater enjoyment of other aspects of life. A person who works too hard is pitied, and the most highly valued kind of work is one that permits independence and does not require working for a supervisor or a boss who gives orders. Work is necessary but not desirable, except insofar as it provides for the basic needs of life.

EMPLOYMENT IN HENDERSON

Henderson began as a combined fishing-farming community, largely self-sufficient with a minimal cash economy. Although both of these enterprises remain important, the economic profile has changed considerably. The fish industry has become a major commercial enterprise, employing many individuals and providing income for many more. Farming, once a small-scale family operation, has also become big business. Today there are no small family farms in the Henderson area despite the fact that most of the land in the area is in active cultivation. Modern technology and equipment, and the economic pressures of the international market, have converted Henderson from an isolated community dependent on itself to a community fully integrated into the international economy.

Much of the income in Henderson is now derived from nonlocal sources. Within the past two decades the oil industry has provided jobs for many young men, who work in capacities ranging from semiskilled roughneck positions to more highly skilled engineering and technical ones. Some of these jobs are within commuting distance (though none within Henderson itself), while others require working on offshore rigs in the Gulf of Mexico or elsewhere. Oil companies offer high pay, especially for minimally skilled workers, and excellent benefits. As a result, these jobs became very popular during the peak of the oil boom, despite difficult working conditions and unpleasant schedules. (Offshore jobs require shifts of 7 or 14 days, during which the workers live on the rig full time, with an equal number of days off during which the workers are at home, sometimes with little or nothing to do.) The infusion of oil-derived money created the greatest increase in the area's prosperity, leading to the heavy emphasis on the acquisition of consumer goods.

These jobs are attractive largely because of the high pay and good benefits, which compensate for the unpleasant working conditions. But some Henderson men have always worked at jobs with similar schedules, and the availability of oil jobs with 7-and-7 schedules did not present young Henderson residents with a novel set of problems. Riverboats along the Mississippi and Atchafalaya rivers have always employed at least some area men, who were forced to leave their families for long periods of time beginning in the 1930s. Arcade Calais worked on a riverboat for a while, as did Nolan Latiolais. In fact, Nolan Latiolais spent so much time working away from home that his daughter, now in her thirties, says her father "worked most of his life in the north, he came home in between but he was there a lot." Henderson is a community accustomed to having its men gone for varying periods of time, and the high pay offered by oil companies has been an attractive inducement for men to take jobs not very unlike those their fathers may have had.

Oil is not the only external source of revenues in the Henderson area, although the prosperity it induced has made many of the other sources possible. Construction work has provided large numbers of jobs as well. During periods of economic prosperity, residential and commercial construction increase, and Henderson residents, with their multiple skills, have long been able to make livings in the building trades. Area men work as contractors, carpenters, carpenter's assistants, and in other capacities on construction jobs, not just in the immediate area but throughout the region. In addition, large oil refinery and other industrial plants within an hour's commute employ various skilled laborers such as electricians, welders, and machinists. Much of this work is related in one way or another to the oil industry, but the jobs, and the income, are derived from other sources and other sets of skills.

There are also several residents of the Henderson area who are employed in various professional capacities in Lafayette or other cities. Many of these people are "outsiders" who have settled in Henderson because of its access to the interstate highway and its rural atmosphere. Among this group are several university professors, real estate agents, and other professionals or business managers. They are the "strangers" long-time residents sometimes complain about. To the extent that they purchase goods and services locally their money, derived from outside, helps keep the economy going. However, they have little other impact on the town.

Women are more likely than men to work locally. With some significant exceptions, women work at wage jobs within easy commuting distance or they work from their homes for home sales companies. Some are managers for area businesses such as restaurants, but in general these businesses are owned by men or owned jointly by a married couple. For the most part women's incomes are secondary to those of their husbands, and these incomes are derived largely from locally based service sector occupations. In addition, the black and Vietnamese residents have not opened businesses and all work for wages in other area businesses. Self-employment in Henderson remains exclusively white and largely male.

Despite the importance men place on self-employment, few in Henderson work full time as farmers. The small family farm, economically viable until this generation, is no longer a feasible way to make a living. Probably the primary reason for this is that economies of scale make it impossible for a small farmer to compete with large agribusiness. The expense of modern equipment requires large-scale operations, much larger than any single landowner can support. This is compounded by the Louisiana inheritance laws, which have converted previously large landholdings into individual plots too small to be worked as private farms. As a result, although most of the land in the Henderson area is farmed, many local landowners find it impossible to make a living by farming their own property.

Instead, farming is now done on a kind of lease or sharecropping system, in which one individual leases the rights to work land belonging to many others. The terms of the leases vary, but ordinarily landowners receive between 20 percent and 30 percent of the proceeds from the farm. By obtaining rights to many plots of land, a farmer can acquire holdings large enough to justify the expense for equipment without having to buy the land outright. Landowners, some of whom have land too small to work as an independent farm, can net some income by having their land pooled with others'. This is especially useful to the many landowners who do not live in the area and who keep their land for investment purposes. It is also helpful for those who wish to keep sizable plots of land intact but cannot or will not farm it themselves. For example, several widows now lease out the land their husbands used to work. In addition, land owned collectively by several heirs to an estate may be leased out to a farmer, if the heirs do not want to subdivide the property into the small plots to which each is entitled. By leasing the farming rights, property owners are guaranteed a steady income without themselves having to work the land. A few men in the area work as farmers, either as principal lease holders or as farmers' helpers, but all work land other than their own in order to make a living from farming.

The successful farmers in the area work many plots of land and operate leases with many different landowners. Even with modern advanced equipment, one person cannot do all of the chores on even a small farm, let alone on the large farms common today. Farmers must hire additional help, especially during harvest season when the crop, usually sugar cane, must be brought in within a restricted period of time. (Louisiana lies just at the northern limits for sugar cane production. Most of the agriculture in St. Martin Parish and the surrounding area is sugar cane, but there are severe time constraints in harvesting. Cane generally is ready to cut in October and must be fully harvested by mid-December, when cool weather can destroy the crop.) Many area men, especially young men without other jobs and unemployed laborers, make seasonal livings as helpers on farms.

Employment in Henderson runs a wide range from independent fishing and home sales work to individual contract labor to highly skilled occupations requiring training and commanding high pay from outside employers. Most of the local jobs demand relatively few skills: fishing, crawfish peeling, waitressing, and similar jobs can be learned quickly and taken up as needed. Most residents with skills and training must work in other communities, but jobs have generally not been hard to find. Because of the independent spirit of Henderson residents, many switch jobs frequently and find their greatest successes when they work for themselves, either as independent contract laborers or as owners of small businesses.

SMALL BUSINESSES

Although many area residents do work for outside employers for varying periods of time, Henderson can be best described as a town of small entrepreneurs. It contains most of the businesses essential to the life of a community: grocery stores, pharmacies, gas and service stations, beauty shops, a hardware store, a bakery, a clothing and sporting goods store, as well as the restaurants and fish plants. All of the businesses are locally owned, most by residents of Henderson itself and a few by residents of adjacent communities such as Cecilia and Breaux Bridge. Two businesses are affiliated with larger chains, but both of these are independent franchises owned and operated by local residents. Although nearby communities contain larger businesses owned and operated by outside chain companies, business in Henderson remains independent, small, and family run.

Henderson contains approximately 50 licensed businesses, a number that has remained relatively constant over the past several years. With just over 500 households in town, this amounts to roughly one business for every ten households. This does not count the many fishers and the few farmers, who are self-employed but not licensed as businesses, nor does it include the independent sales agents, who do not require business licenses. The actual proportion of self-employed persons is therefore considerably higher than the one in ten suggested by the occupational licenses issued by the city. In a very real sense, Henderson is a community of small businesses and independent workers.

This does not contradict the fact that many residents work for oil companies or in other outside firms. In fact, many residents have multiple careers, working for outside employers until they can establish their own businesses. Because oil field jobs require large amounts of time away from home, they are disliked despite the high pay. Men routinely complain about the working conditions in these as well as other jobs and seek to enter business for themselves as soon as they can. For some this occurs after a few years; others work 20 years, take an early retirement, and then set up a business. But for many, the goal of entering business for themselves is a motivating force for much of their lives.

There are many examples to illustrate this pattern. The owner of Peltier's fish plant, a young man who leased the business from the Peltier family for several years before he purchased it outright, worked in a clothing store for several years before he entered the fish-processing business. The Peltier grocery store attached to the fish plant is still owned by the Peltier family and is currently managed by one of the sons. Before he took over the grocery store, the current manager of Peltier's sold cars and owned a bar. Benoit's, the other major grocery store in Henderson, is owned by a man who has worked for most of his life for a railroad company.

It is generally deemed preferable for close relatives to work together. As noted in Chapter 5, Henderson residents often feel that they cannot work with outsiders as well as they can with their family because of potential personality conflicts. Some local businesses are actually partnerships of kin: the Hebert brothers have a construction company; the Breaux brothers jointly lease farmland. In addition, the LeBlanc sisters work together in Wendy's beauty shop; most of the restaurants are operated as family businesses in which many relatives of the owner and/or manager are employed.

The emphasis on employing relatives in family businesses, and the feeling that kin should work together, has resulted in keeping almost all of the businesses in Henderson family concerns. The restaurants, among the largest employers in town, all are managed by relatives of the owners: in some cases the adult children, in others the spouse. All employ relatives of the owner in various capacities, as do the fish plants, the other large employers in town. The smaller businesses, such as the stores, are all owned and operated by close relatives. The hardware store has one regular employee besides the owner: the owner's son. Peltier's grocery employs a son, two daughters, and an older cousin of the original owner; Benoit's grocery is managed by a son of the owner. The result of this is that although many people are on the payroll as employees of these businesses, in fact they are working for family-owned concerns. The son who manages a business may not technically own it, but he is working for his family rather than a "boss," and the business he runs is virtually his own.

The smallest businesses tend to be run as "mom-and-pop" concerns, in which both husband and wife work. This is necessary in a very small business that may not be able to afford to hire help. Businesses such as these are typically ones that the husband is interested in and that he bought or founded. The wife works for her husband in what is essentially his business. For example, there are two mechanic shops owned by the mechanics themselves; their wives operate the cash registers and do the office work, while the husband/owners perform the labor. Although there are some women in Henderson who own very successful businesses (Wendy LeBlanc's beauty shop is one example, as is Pat's Waterfront Restaurant; also there are several successful flower shops and a pharmacy owned by women), in no case does a husband work for his wife in her business. The two female-owned businesses that do employ many relatives and that do provide the major source of incomes for their families were both founded by men and taken over by women: Pat's Waterfront Restaurant, originated by Pat Huval and taken over by his ex-wife, and Peltier's grocery, inherited by Shelton Peltier's daughter when Peltier died. In recent years, daughters have begun to work in family businesses in positions that suggest they might eventually take it over. These younger women, trained in the management of the family business, might eventually bring their husbands and their children into their businesses with them; but this development, if it occurs, lies in the future.

OTHER ECONOMIC ACTIVITIES

Because Henderson residents have always emphasized independence and self-sufficiency, most do not depend on a single source of income for their full support. However good a job, high the pay, or successful a business, most prefer to remain at least partially free from their principal source of income. As a result, there are many secondary economic activities, some of which do not involve cash but contribute directly to the support of the household.

For many, fishing is just such an enterprise. Men who work at other jobs enjoy fishing as a sport and see it as a way to boost their standard of living. Some sell what they catch, making them only marginally different from those fishers who have no other jobs. This is especially the case during periods of high unemployment, when men who usually work for oil companies lose their jobs. During the peak of the crawfish season, unemployed oil field workers, or oil workers on

Private selling of crawfish. Fishers can make more money per pound by selling direct to the public, but they are not guaranteed a sale as they are if they sell to a processor.

their seven days off, fish to raise extra money. Those who are otherwise employed often fish in the early morning before reporting to their regular jobs. In many cases these part-time fishers sell what they catch independently without going through a processor, because the profits are higher and there is no danger of having the income reported. For these people fishing becomes a secondary source of income, a way to help ensure survival and a hedge against hard times.

Although many men sell at least part of what they catch to raise extra money, others keep what they catch for their own consumption. The distinction between a sport fisher who fishes purely for pleasure and one who fishes for the consumption of his family is a fine one. Crawfish, frogs, turtles, and other aquatic animals are routinely caught and consumed by people who have other full-time occupations. This, of course, is also a secondary economic enterprise, because the family can save considerable amounts of money on food if they catch much of what they eat. One woman showed me a photograph of her son in front of a large ice chest full of fish, and said he had caught an ice chest full every day for a week. She was proud of his success as a fisherman (especially because he holds a regular job and is not a commercial fisher), but she was most pleased that the catch would help feed her family for much of the upcoming summer.

Fishing for personal consumption is a vestige of the times when Henderson residents were truly self-sufficient. There are other practices that are also vestiges of this time. Although few residents are professional farmers, many have sizable backyard vegetable gardens. Octave McGee, a retired farmer, keeps a garden that

Vegetable garden in early spring. The owners of this garden are a retired couple who live alone.

resembles a small farm. He produces cabbage, okra, green onions, green peppers, tomatoes, and several other vegetables strictly for the use of his family. He maintains that it is pointless to spend money on food if you can produce it yourself, and that by growing your own food you remain independent. The produce from larger gardens is preserved and used during winter months, and, as with fish, sometimes it is sold for extra cash. Gardening is not the passion that fishing is, and fewer people who raise vegetables sell them. In general gardens are a way to cut food expenses, not a way to earn money.

Although gardens are prized for the food they produce, in some cases gardening is financially disadvantageous. Large gardens especially may occupy land that could be more lucratively used for other purposes, such as real estate development. A successful garden requires a considerable investment in time, time that might be used for more remunerative activities. Nonetheless, many residents prefer to keep their gardens, however counterproductive it may be to do so. Arcade Calais, who still fishes when he wants to, maintains a sizable vegetable garden for the use of his family. He explains that he could make more money fishing than by tending his garden, and that he doesn't keep the garden for reasons of economy:

> But if you don't grow food you'll starve to death with money. You can't eat money, you have to have food, and if you don't grow your own food there's less for everybody to eat.

Bernard and Virginia Dupuis own a large plot of land, some of which is leased as farmland and some of which they work as a garden. Mrs. Dupuis told me that they get requests from people wanting to buy small lots to build houses, but they refuse to sell their land for development. They could make a great deal of money by selling their land or by converting all of it into commercial farmland, but they prefer to raise their own food. As long as they can get by, they would rather keep the land and their garden.

In addition to growing vegetables, several area households raise animals. Formerly most families in the area raised meat as well as vegetables, especially farm families and those with enough land to keep large animals. At regular intervals an animal was butchered, with the meat either distributed among the members of the community or, later, frozen. Today the old-fashioned *boucherie* system, in which families pooled their resources to ensure fresh supplies of meat, is no longer in operation. Instead, the *boucherie* has evolved into a private family affair, with the meat butchered and prepared as before but now stored in a freezer. The concept, however, remains the same: raising animals and butchering provides an ample supply of meat at very little cost. What has changed is simply the substitution of a freezer for a cooperative neighborhood *boucherie* network.

Many area families with sufficient land still raise larger animals such as sheep, cows, and pigs. (This does not count those who keep horses for pleasure use.) In addition to their use in *boucheries*, these larger animals are also kept because they help to maintain the appearance of the yard. Even households without enough land for large animals may keep some smaller ones. Chickens are especially common because they are easy to keep, eat little, and do not require much space. Even families with small plots of land can and do raise chickens for their own

Backyard chickens.

consumption. Few sell either the eggs or the meat, but they consume both and give them away to friends. Irma Davis lives just outside of Henderson on 15 acres of land. She peels crawfish full time and her husband, retired with a pension, fishes and tends a garden. They also raise chickens, cows, and pigs. This household produces most of its own food. Irma explained to me that

> you have to be able to take care of yourself. We're poor people, really, with a lot of kids. We couldn't make it if we didn't have our own food.

As a result of their desire for independence, Henderson residents are able to make money at a number of things besides their regular jobs. Many derive incomes from the lease of farmland, and in the case of several retired couples, farm income provides a substantial proportion of their support. People with sufficient time raise young plants for sale to gardeners early in planting season; housewives sew gift and novelty items for sale in area shops; some people raise horses for sale and/or to race. The tradition of self-reliance makes it possible for residents to survive temporary economic hardships and helps ensure success.

A source of extra income for a Henderson household.

9/Play and other leisure activities

Cajuns may be best known to outsiders for their spirit of play. Indeed, Cajuns of all kinds value their entertainment and they stress the need for and the cultural significance of a "good time." Cajuns frequently describe themselves as people who "know how to have a good time," contrasting themselves with the "rednecks" (north Louisianians), "Yankees" (non-Cajuns), and other Americans who lack that ability. Cajuns take great pride in being people who work hard and play hard. A true Cajun "good time" can be every bit as exhausting as a good day's work.

The ability to "have a good time" is crucial to Cajun identity. In a study attempting to discern what they consider important about their culture, Cajuns from St. Martin Parish named the ability to "have a good time" as the most important of 18 traits in defining modern Cajun identity. This surpassed even the ability to speak French or the possession of French-speaking relatives (Chafetz, Esman, and Manuel 1982). A person who knows how to have a good time and who can sustain a party life while fulfilling life's other obligations is highly respected. It is understood that the young will pursue play somewhat more vigorously than will their elders, but even middle-aged adults with children are expected to be able to have a good time.

Cajuns make a sharp distinction between work and play. Although *coups de main* and other work parties are not uncommon, these are viewed principally as work affairs and only secondarily as entertainment. They do not comprise a "good time." Play, or a good time, is what one does as a respite from the drudgeries of work. One Cajun grandmother described a good time as "anything that gets you away from the hubbub of work." Because it is so important to a well-adjusted life, and because it provides a crucial contrast with the world of work, Cajuns believe that play should be sought as energetically as one pursues one's work.

Although much leisure time is spent in the pursuit of a good time, Cajuns pursue some leisure-time activities that even they do not consider a good time. Some of these can best be viewed as utilitarian activities that overlap rather considerably with work. Craft and repair shops, for example, occupy much of the spare time of men who use these facilities to build and fix household items. When pursued as a hobby, repairs are recreation despite the fact that others in the community may perform the same activities as work. Women sew clothes for themselves and their

32

families, sometimes producing high-fashion wardrobes that they otherwise could not afford. In addition, they sometimes produce craft items, which they may sell to raise extra cash. Fishing is another activity that is work for some and play for others and has utilitarian value. Other popular activities that are not utilitarian but also do not comprise a good time include the relatively recent practice of exercising at local health clubs. Visiting is also common, especially among retired persons and those with irregular work shifts that leave them with large amounts of spare time.

Among the many things Cajuns like to do, gambling ranks high on the list. To a Cajun, life itself is a gamble. All but the youngest are aware of the recent fluctuations in their economy, and they know they have only limited control over their prosperity. The traditional occupations of farming and fishing have always been uncertain enterprises, with climatic fluctuations able to cause great hardship. Henderson residents like other Cajuns remain painfully aware of the economic risks they run from year to year. The hardships inherent in this kind of life have become incorporated into the Cajun world view, and gambling is perceived as a fact of life.

Cajuns will bet on anything with an uncertain outcome. Football games, card games, roosters, horses, politics, and any other aspect of life is subject to betting. The horse races in Lafayette are a popular destination on a night out, and several Henderson residents raise race horses as a hobby. Vacations in Las Vegas have become popular in recent years with the new prosperity. The rise in disposable income within the past generation has increased the amount of money available for gambling, but betting in one form or another has a long history among the Cajuns.

"LAISSEZ LES BONS TEMPS ROULER"

Because traditional Cajun communities were rural and isolated, and because most Cajuns were relatively poor and had little leisure time, opportunities for entertainment were severely limited in the early days. Traditional nineteenth-century forms of entertainment frequently revolved around community dance halls, which were scenes of socializing and opportunities for courtship. As early as 1807, a traveller described Cajun community dances as follows:

> they are no strangers to gaiety. They love to dance most of all. . . . Everyone dances, even *Grandmère* and *Grandpère* no matter what the difficulties they must bear. There may be only a couple of fiddlers to play for the crowd, there may be only four candles for light, placed on wooden arms attached to the wall; nothing but long benches to sit on, and only exceptionally a few bottles of *Tafia* diluted with water for refreshment. No matter, everyone dances (Robin 1966:115).

From that date to the present, commentaries on Cajun life have consistently reported the prevalence of such gatherings (*e.g.*, Perrin 1891; Smith and Parenton 1938; Rushton 1979).

Because Cajun families have always been close-knit, whole families attended these dances, which were often the principal social events of the community. These community dances became known as *fais do dos* (literally "go to sleep") because small children would be put to sleep in a back room while their parents enjoyed themselves. (Today the term *fais do do* has come to refer to a street dance, which may but need not include children and is not a regular part of a community's entertainment.) Other types of community parties broke the monotony of rural life and provided opportunities for social interaction.

In Henderson, the early restaurants also served as dance halls and as the focal point of the community's social life. Until 1960 or so, the eating establishments in Henderson all had dance floors, and the distinction between a nightclub like Broussard's Moonlight Club and a restaurant like Henry Guidry's was a fine one. These were places where families with children could go for a meal, a good time, and to see friends. The community dance hall to which even small children could go was common not just in Henderson but throughout the area in the 1950s.

Today the weekly community dance is defunct, although many communities have dance halls that are active on Saturday nights. Now, however, the dance halls operate as bars, with some regular customers and some irregulars. None functions as a restaurant anymore, and children are no longer allowed in the nightclubs. (In Breaux Bridge, an old restaurant/nightclub was recently reopened in its original form and it has met with great success. However, it is the only combination restaurant/dance hall in the area, and its success is in large part due to its uniqueness.) Today young people prefer to go to the movies ("the show") or to chic, modern nightclubs in other towns, especially in large communities such as Lafayette. Nightclubs with parental supervision are no longer the scene of courtship as they were in the past. However, although the tradition of the communitywide Saturday night dance has died, the tradition of a Saturday night good time has not.

The Cajun philosophy that play is essential to life is captured in three local expressions, all in Cajun French: *lache pas la patate* (literally, "don't drop the potato"), *laissez les bons temps rouler* ("let the good times roll"), and *joie de vivre* ("joy of living"). In its own way each of these indicates the concern for play as well as the realistic assessment that life is replete with difficulties. They reflect the contrast between work and play, but they emphasize the greater importance of the latter.

Although it literally means "don't drop the potato," *lache pas la patate* colloquially means "keep your cool," "stay calm," or "take it easy." This expression is never translated into English but is often injected into an otherwise English conversation. In fact, many young Cajuns are unaware of the translation but use the phrase anyway. The expression is frequently abbreviated to *lache pas* (don't drop), meaningless in both French and English but a convenient shorthand for a phrase well known to all. Most commonly, *lache pas la patate* is used as an informal farewell or as a good-luck message, roughly equivalent to the English "take it easy." It is also used as a way to suggest moral or emotional strength to a person with problems: someone who is very ill, for example, or who has a close relative who is very ill, will be told to *lache pas*. Here the meaning is "be strong," "don't let it get you down."

Lache pas la patate stresses calm in the face of adversity and reflects a general Cajun attitude toward hardship. Every Cajun knows that life is fraught with uncertainty and difficulty. Economic stability in the area has always been dictated by external forces, either the weather or, more recently, the international oil market. Because hardship is a fact of life, there is no point in worrying about it. If you *lache pas la patate*, you will not let circumstances get the better of you; you enjoy life despite the hardships that it brings.

Laissez les bons temps rouler, meaning "let the good times roll," is a logical extension of *lache pas la patate*. Unlike *lache pas*, however, this expression is not often used in everyday speech either in French or in English. Because it is an effective call to play, it is most frequently used to advertise bars or bands. The unspoken implication is that there are bad times to contrast with the good ones, that one should forget one's problems and the bad times and enjoy oneself as best one can. In order to do this one should actively seek entertainment, or the good times.

The overall ethos of play, of *bons temps rouler* and the carefree spirit, is embodied in the expression *joie de vivre*, "joy of living." Like *laissez les bons temps rouler*, this expression is never used in English and only rarely in conversational French. However, it is frequently used in advertising and in popular writings about Cajuns. Cajuns say about themselves that they have a flair for enjoying life, and this is what is implied by *joie de vivre*. While *bons temps rouler* suggests active partying, *joie de vivre* simply indicates that Cajuns know how to find pleasure in life and that they live with an eye toward enjoyment.

It is significant that the domain of play contains the most commonly used expressions in Cajun French. Young Cajuns who do not speak French still refer to *les bons temps* and tell each other to *lache pas*. The mass media emphasize the Cajun fun-loving spirit, which is good for the regional tourist industry, by using these French expressions in advertising. On a superficial level, much traditional Cajun culture has changed considerably in recent years (though on close scrutiny it has changed far less than many imagine), but the fun-loving spirit remains. In this domain the spirit and philosophy of the people has altered little, and the language reflects this continuity.

GOING OUT

To a Cajun, having a good time almost invariably means going out, preferably to a party or a dance. Cajuns acknowledge that, theoretically, a good time can include solitary, sedentary activities such as reading, sewing, watching television, or "whatever you like to do." But they insist that to them such activities are rarely satisfactory. A grandmother living near Henderson noted that, "Around here we're coonasses and we like to go out. If you enjoy something else that's fine, that can be your good time, but really we like to go out."

Going out usually refers to a bar or a dance hall. These are public places that provide the crucial ingredients for a good time: alcohol, a place to get together, and people. Although movies are popular among young people, especially for dates, going to the movies is not generally considered having a good time. Older Cajuns rarely go to movies except to take their grandchildren. A good time is a more active pursuit, in which one makes one's own entertainment in a crowd.

Going out also involves getting dressed up. The grandmother quoted above said that for her a good time is to "get dressed up all ritzy like and go out." Percy Serrette, a bachelor in Henderson, explained that

> all the women set their hair on Friday night. It doesn't matter if they have anything to do on Saturday. But come Friday night they have to set their hair, because you never know what might happen. It just wouldn't be right if it was Saturday night and they hadn't fixed themselves up.

What constitutes being "dressed up" varies greatly according to age, economic status, and personal style. For an old fisherman it may mean putting on a clean pair of pants and a button-down shirt, in contrast to the coveralls or blue jeans he usually wears. For an elderly woman it may mean a new pants suit or a favorite old cocktail dress. Young people, especially women but also men, tend to follow the latest fashions and to have large wardrobes designed for going out. But in any case, getting dressed up is a personal statement that what one is about to do is somehow different from the norm; the appearance of the clothing is less important than the fact of having donned special attire for the purpose of going out.

At the root of a Cajun good time is alcohol. Beer is the Cajun drink of preference, but other alcoholic beverages are also consumed. Cajun children are introduced to alcohol at an early age, as soon as they express an interest in it. The Cajun area has the highest per capita beer consumption rate in the United States. To many Cajuns, a good time can be synonymous with getting drunk, or at least with drinking alcohol. In fact, the study that cited "having a good time" as the most important feature of modern Cajun culture, also showed that "drinks alcohol" is an important trait, especially for the younger generation. This trait was highly intercorrelated with "having a good time," suggesting that one implies the other (Chafetz, Esman, and Manuel 1982). Denise LeBlanc once described a successful weekend of partying: "We stayed drunk for three days."

Getting drunk is, of course, self-reported and difficult to verify, especially because Cajuns are accustomed to drinking large quantities of alcohol and tend to know their own limits. Nonetheless, although it is difficult and impractical to obtain precise measures of drunkenness, Cajuns do value the ability to consume a lot of alcohol while remaining functional. A young woman in Henderson described her previous evening at the grand opening of a bar in Breaux Bridge by recounting in superficial detail the nature of the physical setting; she then went on to explain how good a time she had had. There were, she said, a lot of people there and a good local band. "I woke up with such a headache this morning! I didn't really get drunk last night, but I guess I had a good time."

Although drinking is a major component of Cajun parties and good times, there are individuals who do not care to drink alcohol. Many of these nondrinkers have developed elaborate strategies to disguise this fact. One such strategy is to tell people the next day how drunk you got the night before; you may or may not be believed, but only a person who was present at the event can verify your statements. The young woman who complained of a headache may not actually have had one, but it was expected of her that she should have had a considerable amount to drink and the people (including myself) to whom she was describing the evening were in no position to determine whether she was telling the truth. One man of my acquaintance rarely drinks alcohol, but it was many months and many parties after we met that I learned this. He has developed a carefully staged set of behaviors that make it appear as though he is drinking as much as everybody else. By preparing his own drinks (nobody has to know there is no liquor in his colas) and by altering his demeanor during the course of the evening, he makes it almost impossible for anybody to know how little he really drinks. There is no way to know whether people really drink as much as they say they do, and it is likely that many do not. However, the cultural emphasis placed on alcohol consumption is such that it is expected that people will drink, or that they will pretend to.

Henderson has always had a reputation among surrounding communities as an especially good times town. This may be due in part to the fact that it was founded by a nightclub owner as a place to move his business, and so initially the town contained little more than a bar. In the early years there were as many as three nightclubs at a time in Henderson alone, not counting those in neighboring communities that have always been patronized by Henderson residents. Residents have never allowed obstacles to prevent them from enjoying their good times. During the 1950s Fernand Broussard's Moonlight Club was always crowded, no matter what the weather or other conditions. In 1957 Henderson suffered a flood that left several feet of water standing in the streets. This flood did no severe damage, but it was a great inconvenience and it made travel through the streets impossible except by boat. Denise LeBlanc describes a family photograph of her parents taken during that flood, showing them in a pirogue (a Cajun flat-bottomed boat designed for navigating swamps), on their way to the Moonlight Club. As Denise expressed it, "Nothing was keeping them from going to the Moonlight on a Saturday night!"

When I first arrived in Henderson there were two nightclubs, one owned by Pat Huval and one by a local couple. After a short time Huval converted his nightclub into a restaurant, leaving only a single club in Henderson. In the summer of 1983, that club burned down. For probably the only time in its history, Henderson was without a nightclub, bar, or dancehall. Residents adapted to this loss by patronizing the many clubs in neighboring communities such as Breaux Bridge and Lafayette. Nonetheless, in the summer of 1984 a new nightclub opened within the Henderson city limits, not far from the one that had burned down.*

FUNDRAISERS AND BENEFITS

Although some residents are fairly well-to-do, Henderson remains a working-class community. Self-employed fishers frequently do not possess adequate insurance to cover emergencies such as severe illness. As a result it is easy for families

---

* In the fall of 1984, Pat Huval reopened a nightclub—patterned after the one he had closed several years earlier—in the building vacated when he consolidated his restaurants. This again brought to two the number of such clubs in Henderson, and it underscores the importance of these clubs in the life of the community.

to become victims of unexpected disasters such as illness or fire. A characteristic Cajun response to this kind of hardship is to hold a benefit party for the family in question. Such an event costs each attendee little, provides everybody with a good time, and can net the beneficiary considerable sums of money.

In the fall of 1983 the house of Gerald and Brenda Courville burned to the ground. Within a few days of the fire, friends of the family had posted mimeographed notices throughout the surrounding area announcing a benefit barbeque for the Courvilles. A payment of $3 per person was requested, which entitled the guest to a full meal. The atmosphere was typical Cajun festivity. The Courvilles netted enough money to reestablish themselves, and several weeks after the party they placed an ad in the local weekly newspaper thanking the many people who had attended. Several months later a similar benefit was held to help pay the medical bills of an area man who had both of his legs amputated.

This kind of event is used not only to aid families in need of extra cash, but also to help raise funds for local organizations such as the fire department. There are annual events for the fire department, including parties and softball tournaments. If the price is reasonable and the entertainment good, Henderson residents will pay for a party for virtually any decent cause.

DERIVATION OF THE GOOD TIMES SPIRIT

It is difficult to identify any single cause or group of causes for the Cajun good-times spirit. The age of this culture trait suggests that it derives from culture patterns of the nineteenth century or earlier, but its persistence means that it is a response to current conditions as well. Nineteenth-century Cajun life was, in outline, not very different from that of other rural farmer-fisher peasants of that period. Yet other similarly isolated peasant peoples do not necessarily share the Cajun attitude toward play. The Amish, for example, have long been isolated from the outside and have solved their entertainment problems through parties that explicitly prohibit alcohol consumption; they are not known for their good-times spirit (Hostetler 1968). One aspect that differentiates Cajuns from similar U.S. groups is the nature of their faith: Catholicism. It is likely that the Catholic faith is at least in part responsible for the freedom with which Cajuns have always expressed their exuberance.

It has long been recognized that Catholicism generally permits greater freedom of individual pleasure than do most forms of Protestantism and many other religions (Weber 1930). Catholicism has spawned Mardi Gras celebrations worldwide; an elaborate system of fiestas and saint's day celebrations, especially in Latin America; and many other types of celebrations (Riegelhaupt 1973; Wasserstrom 1978; Boissevain 1969). It has been suggested that Catholics are better able to partake in hedonistic pleasures than are members of other faiths because their church provides mechanisms for them to release their burdens. Confession, which absolves an individual of sins committed; the ability of one person to pray for another; and the fact that the Catholic church permits priests to intercede with God on behalf of a parishioner—all are more conducive to a hedonistic life than are the more stringent rules of Protestantism, in which individuals are responsible for their own salvation. In addition, the Catholic church is somewhat lenient in its policy regarding alcohol consumption. A local Cajun priest explained that Catholics are permitted to drink, in the eyes of the church, until they can no longer tell right from wrong. This allows a person to get quite drunk without overstepping the bounds of religion. That, combined with the ability to go to confession the following day, may be partly responsible for the ebullient Cajun spirit and the emphasis on good times.

Cajuns themselves explain their love of parties and a good time as a function of small-town and fairly isolated living. In the past the only form of entertainment was a party. Weekly gatherings provided a welcome relief from the monotony of everyday family life and the drudgeries of work. These gatherings were among the only ways to keep in touch with neighbors, and the Cajuns claim that continuity has kept the tradition of parties and the good-time spirit alive.

This, however, is only a superficial explanation. Today there are many other forms of entertainment available. Cajuns do not need to depend on a Saturday night dance to stay in contact with their neighbors. Neighbors see each other at home every day, and because of the many clubs and the ubiquity of automobiles, they may not see each other at the clubs that they frequent. There may be some truth to the fact that the love of a party has been passed down from generation to generation, but this is not a wholly satisfactory explanation. In fact, the parties and the good times serve another purpose in modern Cajun communities, a function unnecessary in the past but extremely important today.

Percy Serrette expressed the modern importance of parties as follows:

> Around here it's a small town. Everyone knows everyone. During your life you have feuds with people, you know, disagreements. At a party you can forget about that, it doesn't matter. You can be friends there and it doesn't matter that you might not like each other outside.

Parties, in other words, are a way to ease the tensions that arise as a consequence of living in a small community. Because of the close ties Cajuns have to their homes and their families, this is especially important: moving away to escape social pressure is only rarely a viable alternative. Percy goes on to say that parties serve another purpose as well:

> During the week everybody has a job to do and everybody has a boss. You're not your own man. Come the weekend, you can forget all that, do what you want. What you do is for you, not for someone else. You just let it all out over the weekend because you can't do it all week.

Weekends and parties are temporary respites from the drudgeries of the working world. This is what they have always been, but today they are a respite from taking orders from someone else rather than from the physical hardships of manual labor and poverty. As for alcohol, that too has its purpose:

> When you're drunk, you can say anything and it doesn't count. Everybody understands. You can do things that you can't do otherwise and it doesn't count because you're drunk. So if you want to curse someone out you can. You might get in a fight, but then when it's over and you're not drunk anymore everybody forgets about it.

Parties and alcohol, then, provide a relief from the normal constraints of every-day life in a small town. One can be friends with an enemy, fight with a friend, say things one could ordinarily not get away with, and vent the frustrations that have built up from the week. The pressures of small-town life with its lack of anonymity and the stresses that accrue as a result of seeing the same people every day can be relieved at a weekend party. The good-times spirit therefore has adapted to the changed conditions of the modern world: formerly it provided a source of entertainment, while today it permits the release of frustrations.

FISHING, HUNTING, AND OTHER HOBBIES

Partying, or "having a good time," is only one of many Cajun leisure time activities. Cajuns have a wide range of hobbies, many of which differ little from those of people elsewhere in the United States and some of which are so utilitarian that under other circumstances they might be considered work. Craft and repair shops are hobby activities when they are not a principal source of income, and they are often used as ways to escape the frustrations of work. Several Henderson men enjoy rebuilding old cars or tinkering with engines of various kinds. Women enjoy sewing or crocheting. But in addition to these activities, there are two others that can be considered passions and that consume vast quantities of a Cajun's time, energy, and thoughts. These activities are hunting and fishing. While they are pursued predominantly by men, women sometimes participate; in any event, a wife whose husband hunts or fishes for pleasure is by definition involved in these activities.

Henderson is known throughout Louisiana as one of the better fishing spots, and tourists and weekenders spend a good bit of time there. The area along the Atchafalaya River just outside of Henderson is dotted with weekend camps belonging to people from as far away as Lafayette and Baton Rouge, as well as by locals. There are several stores that sell fresh and artificial bait, fishing gear of all sorts, and sports fishing licenses. Fishing as a hobby is a passion—and because a few local merchants profit from the sports fishers who buy supplies at their stores, it also serves as part of the livelihood for at least a few people in town.

Fishing, of course, remains a major source of employment for many people of Henderson. Most professional fishers pursue that occupation because they like the work and the freedom that accompanies it. For them, fishing cannot be considered a hobby any more than rebuilding old cars can be considered a hobby for a professional mechanic. However, for those men whose livings are made in other ways, fishing is a popular hobby. The ability to navigate the swamps and a knowledge of some of the less accessible but better fishing spots still confers a degree of prestige on a man regardless of what he does for a living. This is especially true for a young man who was not raised in the swamps and therefore had to acquire that knowledge on his own.

Because the area abounds in so many varieties of fish, going fishing in Henderson can mean many things. Most professional fishers devote the bulk of their time to crawfish because that is the most lucrative variety. But the Atchafalaya River contains many kinds of freshwater fish, some of which have commercial value and many of which are eaten domestically regardless of their marketability. Craw-fishing is hard work and is not generally pursued as a hobby (though many non-professional fishers catch crawfish for their own domestic consumption to avoid having to pay for it). The freshwater fish in the river are the source of most of the hobby fishing.

Spring and summer are the seasons when most of the pleasure fishing is done. Many men in the Henderson area own boats and spend their weekends on the river fishing. During these seasons, talk in town revolves around fishing and what kinds of fish are biting where.

Occasionally young women will accompany their husbands or boyfriends on fishing trips, but fishing is generally a male enterprise. I have never known of women fishing for pleasure except in the company of men.

Most commonly, women's involvement with fishing is limited to cooking what the men bring home. Men usually clean the fish, but women are expected to cook it and/or prepare it for freezing. This is sometimes a problem because good fishermen can bring home several coolers full of fresh fish from one trip. While men brag about how much they caught, women complain about how much work they have to do when their husbands go fishing. Angela Guidry, a young woman who works in the office of one of the crawfish-peeling plants, complained one day that after work she had to go home and cook fish all evening. Her husband had gone fishing with his friends for a few days and brought home three large ice chests full of fish, and he expected her to prepare his catch.

Because most people eat the fish that they catch, it is sometimes hard to differ-entiate between fishing as an economic enterprise and fishing as a hobby. The distinction lies in whether the fisher is concerned with repaying the costs of an expedition. Part-time crawfishing in Henderson is frequently performed purely to avoid having to pay commercial prices for crawfish, and is therefore not usually an economic enterprise (but also not technically a hobby because it has an economic purpose). Freshwater fishing, however, requires a greater investment in equipment, and sports fishers rarely concern themselves with repaying the costs of their ventures. Many give away much of what they catch, and so their activities can be perceived only as recreation. This is especially true for retired men, who fish to pass the time and who give what they catch to friends and relatives.

Robert Theriot is a retired mechanic with a comfortable pension. He and his wife Louise live by themselves in a modest house not far from the center of town. All of their five children are grown and live in the area. Robert spends much of his time visiting his friends and relatives and helping his children with odd chores. During crawfish season he fishes as much as he wants, strictly for family use. If his costs get too high, though, he will sell some of his catch in an attempt to break even:

> I do it because I enjoy it. It gives me something to do. We eat it ourselves, us and the kids. I gave most of what I caught last year to my son because he and his wife just had a baby. Before I knew it I spent almost $1000 on bait. So I started to sell some just to make some of that back. I still lost money, but I came out better than I would have otherwise.

As much as Cajun men love to fish, they love hunting more. Cajun men hunt whenever they can, from small game such as duck, rabbit, and squirrel to large game such as deer. Men who have enough money and leisure time make long-distance hunting trips to Mexico, Alaska, Colorado, and other destinations to hunt exotic game. During hunting season men's conversations revolve almost exclusively around hunting, and women joke that their husbands are gone most of the time during the autumn months.

Unlike fishing, hunting cannot be interpreted as an economic enterprise. The cost of equipment is too high, especially given the expense of maintaining camps and dogs. It is true that men may catch large numbers of ducks in a single outing requiring little in the way of equipment, but overall hunting is an expensive luxury. Paul Benoit asserts that his dream is to retire from his business and spend his time hunting and fishing. He says that

> If you do it right you can make enough from fishing to pay for the hunting, and you wouldn't need much extra money because you'd catch most of your own food.

In other words, hunting is an expensive hobby that must be supported by other money-generating activities.

There is probably not a single Cajun man in Henderson who has never been hunting, and there are very few who do not actively pursue hunting as a sport. Boys are given shotguns as soon as they are deemed old enough to shoot, sometimes as early as eight years old. They accompany their fathers and uncles on hunting trips from an early age, and the first major kill represents a kind of informal rite of passage into a man's world. Men hold fond memories of their early hunting trips with their fathers and refer to them often. This may be compounded by the fact that conditions within the Atchafalaya Basin, where most of the local hunting is done, have changed considerably within the past generation. Many men perceive that the hunting was better when they were children. This, however, does not deter them from hunting as often as they can.

Men who hunt frequently generally maintain hunting camps in the Atchafalaya Basin, where they keep their equipment (including dogs) and where they clean and dress their game. Camps are expensive, and most of the land within the basin is owned by large holding companies that will not sell small parcels of land to private individuals. As a result, it is common for groups of men to form hunting clubs, which lease land from the holding companies and share the expenses of building and maintaining the camps. These clubs are usually comprised of relatives and friends, people who would probably hunt together whether or not they shared a camp. Small-scale hunting, however, may be done individually, especially when it does not require the use of camp facilities. More prosperous families may build their own camps. These tend to be more elaborate and are often used for general entertaining as well as for hunting purposes.

Women almost never hunt. Some Henderson area women occasionally accompany their husbands on hunting trips, but this is probably the exception. More often, women may go to the camp, especially if it is being used only by family members and if other women are likely to be present. At the camp, the women perform domestic chores similar to those they perform at home. Sometimes a woman will keep a camp after her husband has died, but she is not likely to hunt there. Camps are generally perceived as male domains, where men can get away from the female-dominated environment of the home.

Because he owns a business, Paul Benoit can take time off almost whenever he wants. During November and December of 1983, Paul took three separate hunting vacations: to Colorado, Montana, and to his camp in the Atchafalaya Basin. During hunting season he often wears his hunting clothes (camouflage pants and jacket and heavy boots) and spends much of his time discussing past and future hunting trips. Paul could sell his business if he really wanted to, so his dream of becoming a full-time hunter and fisher is probably little more than a romantic fantasy, but it indicates how strongly he enjoys hunting and how much he would like to pursue it. Paul's girlfriend wanted to accompany him on his trip to Colorado so she could go skiing. She complained that Paul refused to take time off from his hunting to spend time on the slopes with her, and she did not go with him. When Paul returned from Colorado he spoke proudly of the deer he had killed, but said he had done better the year before and hoped to do better still on his upcoming trip to Montana.

James Calais manages a small business and has less time to spend on long-distance trips than Paul does. He belongs to a club and hunts with his friends on weekends, especially during deer season. During the week he sometimes goes duck hunting in the early morning before he opens up his shop. One November day at lunchtime he boasted of having killed two ducks that morning and said he planned to go out again that afternoon.

Hunting is enjoyed for the sport and for the challenge. Considerable prestige accrues to a man who bags difficult or scarce game. As a result, some men pursue prey out of season or restricted species. The state of Louisiana maintains a staff of game wardens who are responsible for enforcing season, quantity, and game-preservation laws. However, it is not too difficult to circumvent these laws, especially if the game warden in the area is a personal friend. Game-restriction laws are resented in the Henderson area, where people mistrust government and do not like to have their actions regulated or curtailed. On the day he killed the two ducks, James Calais also spoke of having killed some other small game out of season. James has been fined for hunting out of season in the past, and he and his friends resent the controls placed on hunting. They maintain that restrictive hunting laws violate the rights of hunters to pursue their hobby at will.

Although women generally prepare the fish their husbands bring home, they are usually not responsible for cooking game, especially large game. Men clean and prepare their prey at camp and usually do the cooking once they bring it home. Women may cook small game like ducks and rabbits, although men are just as likely to do this. But women are not automatically expected to roast venison, though they may if they so choose. Game animals do not lose as much in freezing as does fresh fish, so the catch need not be prepared immediately. Whereas women may have more work to do than usual when their husbands go fishing, hunting can have the opposite effect.

While men's leisure time tends to take them out of the house, women's hobbies are more likely to be performed at home. Sewing machines are in the home, so women can attend to their children as they sew. Unmarried women and women without children at home may take or teach dance classes, spend several hours a day at a local health club or gym, and visit one another more than do their peers with small children. Even these activities, however, are generally performed when husbands are not at home. It is rare for a woman to leave the house when her husband is there in order to pursue her own hobby. Women are more individually and less passionately involved in their hobbies than are men, and they rarely discuss their hobbies in public.

In sum, Cajun recreational activities range from being highly functional to pure play. The spirit of pleasure, of *joie de vivre*, pervades much of what Cajuns do, but pleasurable activities can sometimes be useful ones. Fishing often contributes to the family food supply; machine shops where men tinker can save on repair bills; sewing can provide the family with clothing that might otherwise be difficult to afford. When pursued for pleasure these activities are not considered work, however functional they may be. A good time, or partying, is the one pleasurable activity that is usually not linked with work, and it is the most important one. The important thing to a Cajun, in Henderson as elsewhere, is to *lache pas la patate*.

10/Henderson and the outside

Although it is a distinct community with a character all its own, the town of Henderson does not exist in a vacuum. It maintains complex relations with its neighboring communities, as well as with the world outside Cajun territory. The contacts Henderson has with people from other areas has affected both the self-image of residents and the way in which they perceive their culture. These contacts, then, are as important to understanding Henderson as are the internal dynamics of life within the town.

RELATIONS WITH NEIGHBORING COMMUNITIES

The two areas with which Henderson is most often contrasted, and with which it has the most contact, are the neighboring communities of Breaux Bridge and Cecilia. Breaux Bridge is by far the largest of the three, and it serves as the commercial and business center for much of the area. Originally the home of much of the merchant elite of the area, Breaux Bridge has traditionally been wealthier than its surrounding rural towns, and many of its residents have a longer history of education and of extensive contacts with the outside world. Henderson and Cecilia both were, and largely remain, farming and fishing towns in which residents have generally been self-sufficient and where education has been less highly valued.

As a result, Breaux Bridge residents tend to think of themselves as more sophisticated than people in Henderson or Cecilia, who are not fully differentiated in their eyes. Henderson and Cecilia are perceived as "country," while Breaux Bridge is "town." (The blurring of the distinction between Henderson and Cecilia is due in large part to the fact that they share a single school system, located in Cecilia, whereas Breaux Bridge has its own schools. Breaux Bridge residents know only that Henderson and Cecilia people are schoolmates and may not know precisely who lives where.) When a professional couple, originally from another state, moved from Breaux Bridge to Henderson in order to save on rent, they were reminded repeatedly by their Breaux Bridge neighbors that they were moving to a country town that lacked sophistication. The neighbors perceived the move as a step down in prestige for the couple involved and wanted to make certain that the implications of the move were fully understood.

For their part, Henderson residents tend to view Breaux Bridge as a community of snobs. They say that Breaux Bridge people view themselves as superior and don't want to recognize that Henderson is not really very different from their town. Henderson residents also point out that their community is a more close-knit one in which people look out for one another, which makes their town better than Breaux Bridge.

The rivalry between Breaux Bridge and Henderson/Cecilia is really the age-old conflict between town and country. This rivalry is dramatized in the annual Breaux Bridge–Cecilia high school football game. The two schools are archrivals, and the football game provides a forum for the expression of hostilities between town and country. (Because the schools are located in Cecilia, Henderson is lumped with Cecilia in the enactment of this rivalry. There is no separate, formal event to dramatize Henderson's own conflicts with its neighbors.) Emotions in all three communities run high for the annual football game, and businesses erect special signs exhorting their team to victory. The students decorate the towns with banners and billboards designed to generate excitement and community pride, and often explicitly to insult the opposing team and community. Adults, long out of school, revive their old school spirit for this game, dress in the colors of their school, and go to cheer on their team. The rivalry is so strong that the games are sometimes followed by petty vandalism, as students play pranks on houses and businesses of the opposing community.

Although Henderson and Cecilia are merged in many eyes because they share a single school system, the two communities perceive themselves as quite distinct. Cecilia is an older town, with origins in the eighteenth century, and it is not located adjacent to the swamp. Its history is one of farming rather than fishing, and some of its families have lived there for many generations. Henderson residents sometimes complain that Cecilia people, like those from Breaux Bridge, look down on Henderson. To a Henderson resident this attitude is especially laughable because in many respects Cecilia is more rural than Henderson is and the differences between the two communities are not as great as those between either community and Breaux Bridge. There is no formal rivalry between Henderson and Cecilia, but residents of either community are quick to correct someone who mistakenly identifies them as coming from the other town.

Most Henderson residents have close relatives living in other communities in the vicinity, especially Breaux Bridge, Cecilia, and elsewhere in St. Martin Parish. Because most of the older generation of Henderson residents were born elsewhere and moved to Henderson, many have siblings who settled in surrounding communities. In addition, children have married and moved to surrounding communities for varying reasons: to live nearer the family of the spouse, to live closer to a job, because they were able to find a more suitable house in another town, and so forth. As a result, it is inevitable that Henderson residents will have direct and often intense contacts with members of other communities.

The conflicts and rivalries among the nearby communities are not expressed among relatives. Residents of Henderson who have close relatives in Cecilia do not perceive significant differences between themselves and these relatives, and vice versa. Comments about residents of these other communities are made with reference to others, not to close relatives of the speaker. The perceptions these communities hold of one another are stereotypes to which exceptions can always be made. In fact, residents of all three communities speak of their friends and relatives in other towns fondly and may not be able to identify individuals who conform to their stereotypes. Nonetheless, the stereotypes hold and persist.

Of the three area towns, Henderson is the one most consistently scorned. Henderson residents may perceive their neighbors as snobs, but their neighbors see them as relatively unsophisticated. A few residents resent the image others have of them and move or desire to move elsewhere to escape it. Most, however, accept this image and adapt to it. The adaptations vary. Some people don't care or consider the characteristics of their neighbors to be undesirable and don't aspire to sophistication anyway. Others rebel, expressing a fierce pride in their swamp background and in the simplicity they are supposed to have. A minority try to upgrade Henderson's image, hoping to rid themselves and their community of their stigma. Whatever the adaptation, Henderson has internalized its image as a backward swamp town, and its residents in one way or another deal with this image that others have of them.

Henderson residents generally prefer living in the country and do not like to spend much time in any urban setting. One local observer maintains that residents have been marked as "country" for so long that they are afraid they might act "wrong" in the city. It is certainly true that Henderson residents think of themselves as country people to whom the city is alien. All area residents shop in Lafayette, some regularly and others more sporadically. Many work and/or play there. But even those who visit Lafayette regularly often complain that they hate to drive in the city and insist they would never want to live there. New Orleans, which is an easy 125-mile drive on the interstate, is genuinely foreign territory. Some residents have never been to New Orleans, and others have gone only a handful of times. Others go when necessary but feel strongly that they do not belong there. One Henderson woman, who owns her own business and is relatively sophisticated, said she hates to go to New Orleans even for a football game and would not go for any period of time:

> I feel closed in by all those buildings. I'm not used to that, not having any space around me. And all those people! I'm just an old country girl, I guess.

TOURISTS AND OTHER VISITORS

The tourist industry is important throughout the Cajun area, and it has played an important role in the retention of Cajun ethnic pride and identity (Esman 1984). Tourism worldwide provides a vehicle for persons of differing cultures to meet. Contacts of this kind cannot help but affect the nature of the host culture, if only because the host group becomes aware that others are interested in them. More specifically, they become aware of which of their culture traits are most interesting to their tourist guests (Smith 1977; Nash 1981). This is especially true with respect to groups accustomed to being mocked for their "backwardness." Visitors to such groups point out a new value in culture traits that previously caused embarrassment. With the advent of tourism, members of such groups begin to recognize and appreciate for themselves the value of what their visitors seek. This has occurred in Henderson, where Cajun culture has become a source of revenue.

Tourists to Henderson arrive on the interstate highway, and billboards along the highway encourage travellers to stop in Henderson to eat. Indeed, tourism on a large scale would be virtually impossible without the interstate because Henderson was so inaccessible before the highway was built. The many small businesses clustered near the interstate exit cater heavily to tourists and other travellers. Gas stations sell Cajun cookbooks, T-shirts, bumperstickers, and other souvenirs. Signs near the exit explicitly welcome tourists and invite their patronage.

This has been the case almost since the interstate exit opened in 1973, but solicitation of tourists increased in 1984 as a result of the Louisiana World Exposition held in New Orleans. Visitors driving to New Orleans from points west had to pass Henderson on the interstate, and many visitors from other areas made special tours through Louisiana after visiting the fair. Businesses in Henderson were quick to recognize the opportunities that such visitors could (and indeed did) bring. Several months before the fair opened, billboards appeared along Henderson's main street welcoming World's Fair travellers to Henderson's restaurants, and electric signs went up issuing similar greetings. None of this would have been possible without the highway.

Sign near the interstate exit just outside of the Henderson city limits.

Tourists rarely stay for more than a few hours because there are no hotel facilities in the area and there is little to see that can be considered a tourist attraction. Along the Atchafalaya Basin levee just south of Henderson are several privately owned boat landings that offer tours of the swamp. These are popular with tourists, who must drive through Henderson to get to and from the boat landings. The tours last only a few hours, though, and do not require an overnight stay. Some of the visitors on the swamp tours stay to eat at a restaurant in Henderson, but many do not, and they have no alternative activities in the community. As a result, tourism is largely (though not entirely) centered within the restaurant industry.

A nearby community within the Atchafalaya swamp contains weekend homes belonging to residents of cities such as Lafayette and Baton Rouge. Many of these weekenders visit Henderson to eat and buy supplies. These visitors return to their weekend homes, however, and except when they eat at Henderson's restaurants they have minimal impact on the community.

Not all of Henderson's visitors come from other parts of the United States or from foreign countries. Many restaurant patrons are Cajuns or non-Cajun residents of area cities such as Lafayette. These people visit Henderson largely for the food and are less interested in local color. They have helped the restaurants and thereby contributed to the rise of a genuine tourist industry in Henderson, but they do not act as tourists because they do not require interpretation of area traditions. Their impact on the town is similar to that of the weekenders: they bring in some outside money, but they do not affect the public presentation of self or Henderson's standing with respect to the outside world.

Most tourists learn about Henderson and Cajuns from their experiences in the restaurants. Chapter 4 discussed the differences between the locally oriented restaurants and the tourist ones: the tourist restaurants present the image Henderson residents believe tourists want to see, whereas the locally oriented ones cater to residents' tastes. It is essential that the restaurants do this because of the importance of the tourist trade.

However, catering to tourists and their interests may require presenting a version of Henderson life that is not entirely accurate. Tourists want to know that Cajuns speak French, but they expect to be served in English. They want to eat local food, but if the food is too spicy they may not like it. They want an elegant atmosphere to match the quality of the food they are served, rather than the simple, family atmosphere that Cajuns prefer. As a result, Cajun culture is interpreted for tourists through the restaurants, which give visitors what they seek.

This is a fairly common pattern around the world among peoples who are no longer culturally "exotic" but who are beneficiaries of tourist industries. Peoples in this position commonly create dual worlds: a "tourist domain" and a "native domain." This permits them to act as the tourists want them to in order to keep the tourist business, while retaining the right to act as they choose in private. Indeed, for many such groups the tourist domain permits the retention of culture traits that might otherwise disappear.

The establishment of a tourist domain sometimes requires people to act more "ethnic" or "native" for tourists than they normally do among themselves. This is the case among native Balinese, who stage public rituals for tourists that fulfill tourists' preconceptions of what Balinese are like, while privately living as Westernized, modern people in a developing economy (McKean 1977). In other cases, as with the Amish, it permits natives to control which aspects of traditional culture they want tourists to witness, in order to protect their cultural integrity (Buck 1978). For the most part, the Cajun establishment of a tourist domain serves the first of these functions: it lets them act more "ethnic" than they usually do and preserves certain aspects of their culture.

The use of French is an important component of the tourist domain both in Henderson and throughout the Cajun area as it highlights the difference between tourist and native domains. Cajuns have never been educated in French, and only those who have made a special effort to learn it can read and write in French. The younger generation, which has limited competence even in spoken French, is more handicapped than are their elders with respect to French literacy. However, tourists to the area are intrigued by its French heritage and want to see evidence that this heritage persists. Yet few tourists can speak or understand French well enough to be served in that language. To resolve this apparent conflict, restaurants and other tourist establishments print French expressions on their menus, advertising, and billboards. Frequently these slogans are misspelled because the people who compose them have had no formal education in the language they are writing. Few natives can read these slogans, but they serve the purpose of highlighting the area's French heritage to tourists. In other words, the written use of French in the tourist domain disguises the fact that many Cajuns no longer use that language, while providing evidence of the French heritage for visitors.

In Henderson, French is used in this way by the tourist-oriented restaurants as well as by other businesses attempting to cater to tourists. In 1984 an area couple, both highly educated and with formal training in French literacy, opened a handicraft shop along Henderson's main road. Believing that many tourists seek to buy locally made handcrafted items, they hoped to attract much tourist business, especially in the light of the World's Fair. They erected a large sign in front of the building with the store's name, "A la Main," which means "handmade." The French name was intended to reflect the heritage of the area and to appeal to tourists. Visitors, who may not have understood the meaning of the name, recognized that the words were French and that they reflected the heritage of the area. In contrast, few Henderson residents realized that the sign was written in French. This was true even for residents who had been raised as French speakers. Most assumed that the words were English and that the name of the shop referred to Main Street, although when the name of the store was read aloud, residents immediately recognized what it meant. Because the business was intended to cater to visitors more than to locals, its owners were more interested in having customers recognize that the name was French than in having the words understood. By giving the store a French name, the owners disguised the local decline in the use of French and provided tourists with the desired image of an exotic culture.

Because tourism is focused around Henderson's restaurants and a few other small

Store opened in Henderson to capitalize on the tourist trade. Note sign in French.

businesses, many area residents have little or no contact with these visitors. Fishers, housewives, most crawfish peelers, people who work outside of Henderson, and many others are not directly influenced by the presence of so many visitors. Yet their lives are indirectly affected because of the nature of the businesses in their town and because of the constant reminders that there is tourist interest in them and in their community. In 1983 one of Henderson's restaurants hung a banner expressing support for Cecilia's football team during the weekend of the Breaux Bridge–Cecilia game. This banner virtually covered the front of the restaurant building. A Henderson housewife complained to me about the banner, on the grounds that it might look bad to the tourists. She was proud that the restaurant was publicly supporting the local team, but she was concerned about the public image such a sign would present. She herself was not affected by the presence of the banner, but she did not want her town to convey a bad impression. (This also indicates the contrast between tourist and native domains in Henderson. The football game is important in the native domain, but this woman considered it to be inappropriate for tourists to be exposed to this aspect of the local culture. She wanted her town to look dignified for the tourists and to reserve such things as local football game rivalries for private contexts.)

Henderson residents are proud that visitors are interested in them. Sometimes, however, they mock tourists' ignorance of the area. This is especially true when they perceive that their visitors expect Cajuns to be wild and culturally backward. I have never known of a tourist being insulted by a local or being mocked directly. However, residents sometimes joke privately about the expectations outsiders have of them. For instance, a group of tourists visiting one of Henderson's crawfish plants asked the manager where they could find some Cajuns. He laughed as he recounted the story:

> They asked me where they could see a Cajun. I told them "You're looking at one." I told them everybody around here is a Cajun. They couldn't believe it—like they thought a Cajun was some kind of savage or something. I don't know what they expected. They were nice people, polite and everything. They just couldn't believe that we would just be people like anybody else.

This man was not insulted by his visitors, but he found their ignorance amusing.

Although tourists are always treated politely and with respect, and although everybody recognizes the value of the tourist industry, tourists have become a factor in local conflicts. The main street of Henderson has several sharp curves along its three-mile length, and the speed limit on this one road changes several times. During one of Henderson's budgetary crises, the police chief asked his officers to enforce the town's speed limits more rigorously than they had been, and as a result many speeding tickets were issued. The mayor objected to this practice on the grounds that issuing tickets might scare away the tourists. The chief claimed he was only trying to enforce the law and to increase the town's money supply; the mayor countered that scaring away the tourists would hurt both the town and its citizens by costing sales tax revenues and jobs. (Few local citizens were affected by the speeding tickets. Local kinship and friendship ties work in favor of town residents because most people can claim a favor from the officer on duty, the chief, or the mayor. Also, most residents live within the last mile or so of the road, making it difficult for them to get up enough speed to warrant a ticket.) The chief did not oppose the tourist industry, but he maintained that visitors should not be treated with special consideration. Eventually the speeding tickets ceased to be issued, and the controversy died down. To my knowledge, this is the only time the tourist industry was involved in a public controversy. Nonetheless, this one case indicates that there is disagreement over how the tourists should be treated and that there may be some potential for conflict.

Tourists and other restaurant patrons are welcomed in Henderson and have helped instill a sense of pride among many residents. Other outsiders, however, are not quite so welcome. Visitors who do not fit the tourist pattern are often suspected of having evil intentions, and they are certainly questioned. Researchers, for example, may not be well received unless they are known in the community (or unless they speak French, in which case it is assumed they are not out to exploit anybody). This posed little problem for me because I was able to build up contacts slowly. People doing survey research, in which they visit each household for a short period of time and have no extensive contacts in the community, find Henderson a difficult place to work because many residents refuse to participate. After many years of being exploited and mocked by outsiders, residents have learned to protect themselves by refusing to deal with outsiders whose motives are not completely clear.

OUTSIDERS AND HENDERSON'S SELF-IMAGE

Henderson's self-image is a contradictory blend of inferiority, derived from the town's reputation among its neighbors, and pride, derived from the tourists. Both of these images are the result of the swamp background and the strength of Cajun culture in the area. Henderson residents enjoy the fact that they are of interest to non-Cajun visitors. However, those residents whose lives are more directly affected by their relations with surrounding communities continue to perceive themselves as the backward swampers of the area. They are not necessarily ashamed of this, they have merely accepted their ranking in the area hierarchy of communities.

The apparent contradiction between these two perceptions of self can be explained by the nature of relations with the two categories of outsiders. Tourists, who instill pride, are transients by definition. None stays long enough to establish a relationship with local people or to understand the true nature of the community. The opinions of tourists are derived from the public image that Henderson residents choose to present. Neighbors in nearby communities are in a better position to evaluate the nature of the town, and many maintain permanent relationships with Henderson residents. Permanent or long-term relationships with neighbors of necessity take precedence over the temporary ones between Henderson hosts and individual tourists. Although residents are proud that their visitors find them interesting, they must still live with the scorn of their neighbors, with whom their lives are genuinely intertwined.

As a result, Henderson is simultaneously proud and a little bit embarrassed. It welcomes outsiders whom it can control but is less enthusiastic about those it cannot. Its residents avoid contact with urbanites in urban territory, where they are not in control and where they feel out of place. The future of Henderson's self-image is linked with both kinds of outsiders, neighbors and tourists. This future will be determined by the way in which the community can integrate these two facets of its identity.

11/Conclusion: culture change and the survival of ethnic identity

This study has discussed many aspects of life in a single small community, attempting to describe how one group of people is managing its transition from traditional peasant ways to participation in the wider U.S. culture. Henderson is only one of many Cajun communities, and it does not fully represent them all. However, in many ways it illustrates patterns that have occurred not just in Louisiana but elsewhere in the world since World War II. Economic development and technological advances since that time have brought many formerly isolated, culturally and linguistically distinct peoples into the mainstream. One result has been an increase in assimilation and an apparent demise of traditional culture traits (see Glazer and Moynihan 1975).

At the same time as they have been abandoning their traditional cultures, many of these groups remain faithful to their ethnic identities. This is manifested in a concern for the history of cultural differences, in an insistence on a separate ethnic classification, in a preservation and sometimes a revival of old culture traits including language, and in some cases by asserting the rights to political sovereignty. Hence in Wales there is now a movement to introduce the teaching of the Welsh language, which is all but defunct; similar movements are afoot in Brittany and elsewhere. The Basques of Spain and France seek not only a cultural revival but political autonomy as well, and political separatism is a recurring theme in Quebec. It appears that change in culture content need not require the loss of identity, nor does it necessarily entail a lack of interest in traditional culture.

These issues have sparked tremendous scholarly and political interest and debate in the past two decades. Volumes have been written attempting to explain the increase in ethnic activity that has coincided with the decline in traditional cultures (*e.g.*, Glazer and Moynihan 1975; Esman 1977; van den Berghe 1981). Many observers mourn the apparent loss of ethnic diversity that has accompanied technological modernization. These observers have equated culture with identity, assuming that without a separate culture it is impossible to maintain a separate identity. As a result, they find it surprising that groups can be interested in their identities while changing their cultures, and they seek ways to preserve indigenous culture traits in order to protect the identity.

However, anthropologists have long recognized that culture and identity are not coterminous. Cultures change regularly, and peoples have long been faced with changing cultures and constant identities. It is true that in some cases the changes

127

are more heavily influenced by members of other groups, which frequently results in assimilation to an outside cultural system rather than simply change within a traditional one. But this does not necessarily render the resulting product less "authentic" than if outsiders were not involved, nor do the possessors of the culture in question necessarily abandon their sense of identity just because they adopt traits from outside. The key to the survival of group identity lies not in whether its members remain faithful to an antiquated set of behaviors, or whether they avoid all influences from outside. Both of these conditions are impossible. Rather, ethnic survival consists in whether a group can incorporate new developments into its identity. If people continue to consider themselves to be members of a given group despite changes in their culture, then the group maintains its integrity (Barth 1969).

These patterns have occurred among the Cajuns. While Cajun culture has changed, Cajuns retain a profound sense of themselves as a people apart. Regardless of the degree of assimilation—and this varies widely from one community to another and from one individual to another—Cajuns know that they have a special heritage not shared by their neighbors. They insist on being known as *Cajuns*—as opposed to Yankees, Americans, rednecks, Texans, and others—despite the many superficial similarities to their neighbors elsewhere in this country. Cajuns in Henderson affiliate with "Americans" only when compared with their Vietnamese neighbors, who are less "American" than themselves; otherwise they identify strongly as Cajun regardless of their behavior.

Yet Cajuns do not desire to return to their former ways. They recognize that many aspects of their culture have changed over the years to adapt to the conditions of the modern world, and they know that their best interests lie in some degree of assimilation. But Cajuns, as others in their position, see little conflict between changed culture and constant identity. They continue to identify as Cajuns because of a heritage that remains significant regardless of the culture traits that accompany it. As a result, whatever the future of specific traditional Cajun culture traits, Cajun identity should remain strong and durable.

At the same time, many Cajuns are concerned that their traditional culture may be dying. Elderly Cajuns sometimes complain that their grandchildren don't speak French, and they maintain that the loss of their traditional language signals the loss of a cultural system. Yet some old traits that have been on the decline—notably the use of French—are being revived as symbols of a separate identity. They are now used in contexts in which their symbolic value may outweigh their functional value, such as in tourism and local politics. They serve as reminders to everybody of a separate tradition and heritage that may be less visible in other aspects of life. Louise Theriot is a grandmother who acknowledges that her grandchildren do not speak French and do not adhere to many of the traditional Cajun ways. But she does not regret their inability to speak French because she believes that French is of little use to them in the modern world. She recognizes that the culture is changing and that the demands placed on its members are not the same as they once were. She can accept that her grandchildren are Cajuns, but in a different way than she is. Being Cajun in Henderson means having a heritage, regardless of current behavior, and it also means sharing a set of cultural symbols that may have little more than symbolic value.

This is a common pattern around the world. Few of the groups involved in ethnic activity desire to return to the old ways. Instead, ethnic groups are reasserting their identities through symbols, despite their changed culture. They do this in an attempt to demonstrate that they can remain viable groups regardless of the nature of their culture. In Wales the attempt to teach Welsh is not at the expense of English—it is in addition to English, which is widely viewed as essential. In Louisiana the new interest in French is likewise as a second language. The traits that are revived are perceived as symbols of group heritage and are valued for their symbolic significance more than for their practical value.

Tourism is one vehicle through which the symbols of ethnic identity can be expressed. It can contribute to a resurgence in ethnic pride by bringing in visitors willing to pay to witness native culture. This often creates a new interest in otherwise dying culture traits and helps perpetuate, at least in a tourist domain, traits that may otherwise disappear. This has occurred in Gozo, Malta (Boissevain 1979), as well as in Bali (McKean 1977), and as this study has shown, it has also occurred among Cajuns in Henderson.

The dual domains of the tourist industry permit Cajuns in Henderson and across Louisiana to preserve certain aspects of their traditional culture that might otherwise have little value in the modern world. This is especially true with respect to those traits that are most easily exploited for their symbolic value. As the younger generation ceases to speak French, that language is losing its position as the language of local commerce. Yet because visitors want to witness the use of French, it may be preserved in tourist contexts—which will require at least some local residents to be able to use that language.

A similar situation holds with respect to Cajun music, which is unique to the area. Traditionally, Saturday night dances in Cajun communities featured local bands who played the local kind of music. Recently Cajun music has declined in popularity among locals, who prefer rock and roll or country and western. The dance halls that cater to elderly Cajuns today feature bands that play combinations of Cajun and country. Yet Cajun music is enjoying a renaissance of popularity among outsiders. Breaux Bridge contains two dance halls featuring Cajun music, both of which attract large numbers of tourists and other visitors. In Henderson, all of the restaurants sell records of Cajun music, but it is the tourists and not the locals who buy them. The current success of Cajun music is also exclusively a product of outside interest, and were it not for the area's tourist trade, there would be little work for even the most popular Cajun bands.

In many respects, Cajun culture in Henderson has changed less than it might seem to have at first glance. Family units remain strong and kin continue to live adjacent to one another. The family remains largely responsible for the perpetuation of Cajun culture. Many traits persist within the family context and are linked with men more than with women. These traits are the private ones, the ones that require the transmission of attitudes, philosophies, and world view. In addition, the traditional occupation of fishing persists and flourishes, as does an old pattern of men working away from home for long periods of time. The spirit of self-sufficiency continues to govern much of what people do. The good-times spirit thrives in area nightclubs, at parties, and in a general attitude toward work and life. The community remains philosophically egalitarian despite what are now rather marked discrepancies in income. These patterns are old, they are fully ingrained in the life of the community, and they are not likely to disappear in the near future.

However, these traits are not readily recognizable to outsiders. In fact, the traits that remain most faithful to old patterns are the ones that are private, while the ones that have changed are the ones that are most conspicuous. Visitors to the area cannot know that siblings are also neighbors, nor can they know how people think about their jobs, their money, or their free time. They certainly cannot discern the complex ways in which old attitudes permeate what appear to be modern customs. Cajuns themselves may not be fully aware of how much their current behavior resembles their traditions. They see media reports of the decline of traditions, such as the use of French, and they see the external trappings of their lives come to resemble those of people across the United States. Television and other media do a lesser job in recording attitudes and philosophies, so many Cajuns do not realize how much they still differ from other U.S. citizens in terms of their basic attitudes toward life. For this reason Cajuns, as many others in similar situations, have developed a public display to highlight disappearing aspects of their culture for the benefit of visitors (and to remind themselves of where they came from).

In Henderson, Cajun culture survives in an updated form, and current trends suggest that it will not be fully supplanted by urban U.S. mainstream culture. Television, cars, fashionable clothing, and even the use of English are merely external trappings, a veneer covering more traditional attitudes. It is perhaps for this reason that Henderson has remained largely indifferent to the activities of the Lafayette-based ethnic revival organizations: in Henderson Cajun culture does not need to be revived. Residents *ont pas lache la patate*—they have not given up on their culture or their identity. Because Henderson residents can accept as authentic updated versions of their own traditions, they do not fear for their identity.

This does not mean that ethnic identity is not an issue in Henderson. I hope I have illustrated that it is very much an issue there. In a town like Henderson, as in other similar communities around the world, ethnic identity cannot help but be an issue. It is used and manipulated for personal ends by clever politicians who introduce their speeches in French and who appeal to "our way of life" in their campaigns. It is similarly used by the restauranteurs and other participants in the tourist economy who offer what the tourists want in order to increase their own successes. But Henderson is comfortable with its dual domains and the current nature of its own identity. Its residents do not worry much about their future.

The story of Henderson is an ethnic success story because it illustrates that technological modernization need not signal the demise of either traditional culture or a separate identity. This is important in the light of current scholarly and poli-

Cajun identity remains strong and viable in Henderson, linked with the current nature of life in the community.

tical concerns suggesting the contrary. If observers of ethnic phenomena worldwide would recognize, as do the people of Henderson, that change can be incorporated into both culture and identity, they would be far less worried about the ultimate loss of ethnic diversity.

References

Acheson, James M., 1981, "Anthropology of Fishing," *Annual Review of Anthropology*, 10:275–316.

Barth, Frederik, 1969, "Introduction," in Frederik Barth (ed.), *Ethnic Groups and Boundaries*. Boston, Little, Brown.

Boissevain, Jeremy, 1969, *Saints and Fireworks: Religion and Politics in Rural Malta*. London School of Economics Monographs on Social Anthropology, no. 30. London, Athlone Press.

——, 1979, "The Impact of Tourism on a Developing Island: Gozo, Malta," *Annals of Tourism Research*, 6(1):76–90.

Buck, Roy C., 1978, "Boundary Maintenance Revisited: Tourist Experience in an Old Order Amish Community," *Rural Sociology* 42(2).

Chafetz, Michael D., Marjorie R. Esman, and Marcella Manuel, 1982, "Cajun Ethnicity: A Quantitative Approach," Presented to the Southern Society for Philosophy and Psychology, Fort Worth, Tx.

Comeaux, Malcolm, 1972, *Atchafalaya Swamp Life*. Baton Rouge, La., State University Press.

Esman, Marjorie R., 1984, "Tourism as Ethnic Preservation: The Cajuns of Louisiana," *Annals of Tourism Research*, 11(3): 453–467.

Esman, Milton J. (ed.), 1977, *Ethnic Conflict in the Western World*. Ithaca, N.Y., Cornell University Press.

Glazer, Nathan and Daniel P. Moynihan (eds.), 1975, *Ethnicity: Theory and Experience*. Cambridge, Harvard University Press.

Gluckman, Max, 1955, *Custom and Conflict in Africa*. Glencoe, Ill., Free Press.

Gold, Gerald R., 1978, "*Cousin* and the *Gros Chiens*: The Limits of Cajun Political Rhetoric," Projet Louisiane Working Paper no. 1. Toronto, York University (Xerox).

Griffin, Harry L., 1950, "The Acadians in Louisiana," *Proceedings of the Annual Geneaological Institute*, Baton Rouge.

Hicks, George L., 1976, *Appalachian Valley*. New York, Holt, Rinehart and Winston.

Hostetler, John A., 1968, *Amish Society*. Baltimore, Johns Hopkins University Press.

La Caze, Cecil, 1976, *Crawfish Farming*. Baton Rouge, Louisiana Wildlife and Fisheries Commission.

Longfellow, Henry Wadsworth, 1847, *Evangeline*. Boston, William D. Ticknor & Co.

McKean, Philip Frick, 1977, "Towards a Theoretical Analysis of Tourism: Economic Dualism and Cultural Involution in Bali," in Valene L. Smith (ed.), *Hosts and Guests: The Anthropology of Tourism*. Philadelphia, University of Pennsylvania Press.

Nash, Dennison, 1981, "Tourism as an Anthropological Subject," *Current Anthropology* 22(5):461–81.

Newton, Milton B. Jr., 1972, *Atlas of Louisiana*. Baton Rouge, School of Geoscience, Louisiana State University.

Perrin, William Henry, 1891, *Southwest Louisiana Biographical and Historical*. New Orleans, Gulf Publishing Co.

Pirtle, Caleb, 1977, "Cajun Country," *Sky* (Delta Air Lines), 6(9).

Reed, Roy, 1976, "The Cajuns Resist the Melting Pot," *New York Times Magazine*, February 29.

Riegelhaupt, Joyce, 1973, "Festas and Padres: The Organization of Religious Action in a Portuguese Parish," in Susan T. Freeman (subed.), "Studies in Rural European Social Organization," *American Anthropologist*, 75(3).

Robin, C. C., 1966, *Voyage to Louisiana 1803–1805*, Stuart O. Landry, trans. New Orleans, Pelican Publishing Co.

Rushton, William Faulker, 1979, *The Cajuns*. New York, Farrar, Straus & Giroux.

Service, Elman, 1975, *Origins of the State and Civilization*. New York, W. W. Norton.

Smith, T. Lynn and Vernon J. Parenton, 1938, "Acculturation and the Louisiana French," *American Journal of Sociology*, vol. 44.

Smith, Valene, 1977, "Introduction," in Valene L. Smith (ed.), *Hosts and Guests: The Anthropology of Tourism*. Philadelphia, University of Pennsylvania Press.

Statistical Abstract of Louisiana, 1981. New Orleans, University of New Orleans and Louisiana State Planning Office.

Tentchoff, Dorice, 1977, "Speech in a Louisiana Cajun Community," Ph.D. dissertation, Case Western Reserve University.

U.S. Census of Population, 1980, Washington, D.C., Government Printing Office.

van den Berghe, Pierre L., 1981. *The Ethnic Phenomenon*, New York, Elsevier.

Wasserstrom, Robert, 1978, "The Exchange of Saints in Zinacantan: The Socio-economic Bases of Religious Change in Southern Mexico," *Ethnology*, 17(2).

Weber Max, 1930, *The Protestant Ethic and the Spirit of Capitalism*. G. Allen & Unwin.

Index